THE ENTITY-RELATIONSHIP APPROACH TO LOGICAL DATABASE DESIGN

Books and Training Products From QED

Database

Data Analysis: The Key to Data Base Design
The Data Dictionary: Concepts and Uses
DB2: The Complete Guide to Implementation and Use
Logical Data Base Design
DB2 Design Review Guidelines
DB2: Maximizing Performance of Online Production Systems
Entity-Relationship Approach to Logical Data Base Design
How to Use ORACLE SQL*PLUS
ORACLE: Building High Performance Online Systems
Embedded SQL for DB2: Application Design and Programming
Introduction to Data and Activity Analysis
ORACLE Design Review Guidelines
Using DB2 to Build Decision Support Systems
IMS Design and Implementation Techniques
SQL for DB2 and SQL/DS Application Developers
Using ORACLE to Build Decision Support Systems
Database Management Systems: Understanding and Applying Database Technology
Effective DSS Processing with Teradata

Systems Engineering

Handbook of Screen Format Design
Managing Software Projects: Selecting and Using PC-Based Project Management Systems
The Complete Guide to Software Testing
A User's Guide for Defining Software Requirements
A Structured Approach to Systems Testing
Storyboard Prototyping: A New Approach to User Requirements Analysis
The Software Factory: Managing Software Development and Maintenance
Data Architecture: The Information Paradigm
Advanced Topics in Information Engineering
Software Engineering with Formal Software Metrics
Data Architecture: An Information Systems Strategy (Video)

Management

CASE: The Potential and the Pitfalls
Strategic and Operational Planning for Information Services
The Management Handbook for Information Center and End-User Computing

Management (cont'd)

Winning the Change Game
Information Systems Planning for Competitive Advantage
Critical Issues in Information Processing Management and Technology
Developing the World Class Information Systems Organization
How to Automate Your Computer Center: Achieving Unattended Operations
Ethical Conflicts in Information and Computer Science, Technology, and Business
Mind Your Business: Managing the Impact of End-User Computing
Controlling the Future: Managing Technology-Driven Change

Data Communications

Data Communications: Concepts and Solutions
Designing and Implementing Ethernet Networks
Network Concepts and Architectures
Open Systems: The Guide to OSI and its Implementation

IBM Mainframe Series

How to Use CICS to Create On-Line Applications: Methods and Solutions
DOS/VSE/SP Guide for Systems Programming: Concepts, Programs, Macros, Subroutines
Systems Programmer's Problem Solver
VSAM: Guide to Optimization and Design
MVS/TSO: Mastering CLISTS
MVS/TSO: Mastering Native Mode and ISPF
Advanced VSE System Programming Techniques
REXX in the TSO Environment
DOS/VSE: Introduction to the Operating System

Self-Paced Training

SQL as a Second Language
Building Online Production Systems with DB2 (Video)
Introduction to UNIX (CBT)
Building Production Applications with ORACLE (Video)

Programming

C Language for Programmers, Second Edition
VAX/VMS: Mastering DCL Commands and Utilities

For Additional Information or a Free Catalog contact

QED Information Sciences, Inc. • P. O. Box 82-181 • Wellesley, MA 02181
Telephone: 800-343-4848 or 617-237-5656

The Entity-Relationship Approach to Logical Database Design

Peter Chen

QED Information Sciences, Inc.
Wellesley, Massachusetts • Montreal

© 1977, 1991 by QED Information Sciences, Inc.
170 Linden Street
Wellesley, Massachusetts 02181

All rights reserved. No part of the material protected by this copyright notice may be reproduced or utilized in any form or by any means, electronic or mechanical, including photocopying, recording, or by any information storage and retrieval system, without written permission from the copyright owner.

International Standard Book Number 0-89435-384-5

Printed in the United States of America

91 92 93 10 9 8 7 6 5 4 3 2 1

Contents

Preface ix

Acknowledgements xi

Chapter 1 — Introduction 1

    1.1 Basic Terminology   1
    1.2 Logical Database Design and Physical
        Database Design   4
    1.3 Database Systems and Data Models   6
    1.4 Problems in Logical Database Design   7
    1.5 A New Approach to Database Design:
        The Entity-Relationship Approach   10
    1.6 Advantages of the Entity-Relationship Approach   10

Chapter 2 — E-R Approach and ANSI/X3/SPARC 13

    2.1 ANSI/X3/SPARC Proposal   13
    2.2 Conceptual Schema and Enterprise Schema   14
    2.3 Three Types of Administrators of Databases   18
    2.4 Relevance to the E-R Approach   19

Chapter 3 — Entity-Relationship (E-R) Diagram 21

    3.1 Entities and Relationships   21
        3.1.1   Entity Type   21
        3.1.2   Relationship Type   21

3.2 Descriptions of Entities and Relationships   26
    3.2.1   Attributes and Values   26
    3.2.2   Entity Identifier   27
    3.2.3   Relationship Identifier   28
3.3 Special Entity and Relationship Types   29
    3.3.1   Existence Dependency   29
    3.3.2   ID Dependency   29

Chapter 4 — Translation of E-R Diagrams into Data-Structure Diagrams 33

4.1 Data-Structure Diagrams   33
4.2 Translation Rules   38

Chapter 5 — Steps in Logical Database Design and Examples 45

5.1 Major Steps in Logical Databse Design   45
5.2 Example 1: A Manufacturing Company   45
    5.2.1   Identify Entity Types   45
    5.2.2   Identify Relationship Types   46
    5.2.3   Draw an E-R Diagram with Entity and Relationship Types   48
    5.2.4   Identify Value Types and Attributes   48
    5.2.5   Translate the E-R Diagram into a Data-Structure Diagram   52
    5.2.6   Design Record Format   53
5.3 Example 2: An Order-Entry Database   59
    5.3.1   Identify Entity Types   59
    5.3.2   Identify Relationship Types   59
    5.3.3   Draw an E-R Diagram with Entity and Relationship Types   60
    5.3.4   Identify Values, Types, and Attributes   60
    5.3.5   Translate the E-R Diagram into a Data-Structure Diagram   61
    5.3.6   Design Record Format   62
5.4 Example 3: A Library Database   62
    5.4.1   Identify Entity Types   62
    5.4.2   Identify Relationship Types   64
    5.4.3   Draw an E-R Diagram   65

5.4.4 Identify Attributes and Value Types 65
5.4.5 Translate the E-R Diagram into a
Data-Structure Diagram 66
5.4.6 Design Record Format 66

Chapter 6 — Other Considerations in Logical Database Design 71

6.1 Other Translation Rules from E-R Diagrams
to Data-Structure Diagrams 71
6.2 Modify the Data-Structure Diagram for Performance
and Storage Reasons 72

Chapter 7 — Design of Hierarchical Databases 77

7.1 Translation Rules 77
7.2 Example 78

Chapter 8 — Final Remarks..81

References 83

Preface

The Entity-Relationship Approach provides an easy to understand yet comprehensive methodology for logical database design independent of storage or efficiency considerations. In this monograph, the use of Entity-Relationship diagrams is explained, along with rules and examples for translation into hierarchical or network structures. A comprehensive example using a manufacturing application is provided.

Acknowledgements

The author wishes to express his thanks to the following persons for their assistance in developing the Entity-Relationship Approach:

Garry Norris, Max Wilson, Gale Shirk	Cummins Engine Company
Kort Peters, Ann Tindel	Stop and Shop Companies
John Haaland, Sara Read	Pillsbury Company
Chander Ramchandani, James Iverson, Philip Sherman	Xerox Corporation
Robert S. Howard, Thomas McGinty, Chuck Brush, Ken McNeil	Foxboro Company
Paul Saia, Jr.	M.I.T.'s Office for Administrative Information Service

The author also would like to thank the following students for their assistance and suggestions: Michael Chang, Jacob Akoka, Arnold Schiemann, Larry Brooks, Marty Palka, Don Schulsinger, John Andoh, Kwok Cheong Lee, Scott McDermott, and Deborah Cohen.

The guidance and encouragement of Dr. John Rockart, Director of the Center for Information Systems Research at M.I.T., made this work possible. The author also would like to thank Dean William Pounds, Dean Michael Scott-Morton, Professor John Little, Professor Stuart Madnick, and Professor John Donovan of the Sloan School for their encouragement.

The support from the National Science Foundation, the Center for Information Systems Research, and the Undergraduate Research Opportunities Program at M.I.T. is especially appreciated.

Finally, the author would like to thank his wife, Li-Chuang, for her patience and encouragement during the preparation of this monograph.

Introduction 1

The management of data has become one of the most important activities in many organizations. As we move to an increasingly information-oriented society, determining how to organize the data to maximize their utility becomes a very important problem. Computer-based file systems and database systems simplify the task of maintaining and retrieving a large quantity of data. However, the problem of how to organize the data to utilize the full capability of the file or database system is not well understood by many data processing people. The purpose of this monograph is to provide a methodology which makes the process of organizing data easier to understand and follow.

1.1 BASIC TERMINOLOGY

In this section, we shall explain several basic concepts in data management.

A *record* is a collection of data items. For example, an EMPLOYEE record contains the data relevant to a particular employee (Figure 1). A record is divided into several *fields*. In Figure 1, NAME, SALARY, and ADDRESS are the names of the fields of an EMPLOYEE record. Field names are used to interpret the meaning of the data items (or *values*) in the record. Therefore, "ROBERT JOHNSON" is the "NAME" of a particular employee, and "10K" is his "SALARY." A *file* is a collection of records of the same type. For instance, the EMPLOYEE file is a collection of EMPLOYEE records (Figure 2).

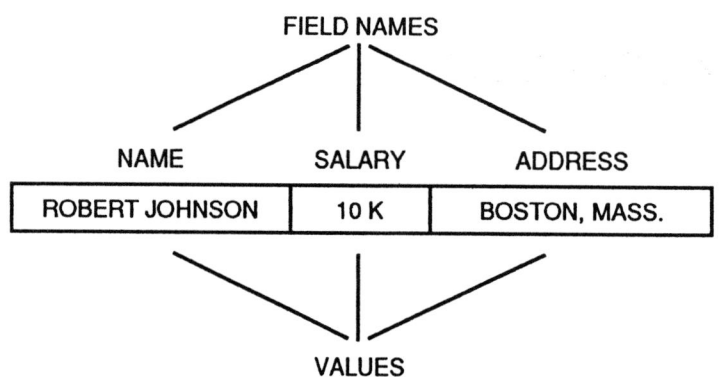

Figure 1. An EMPLOYEE record.

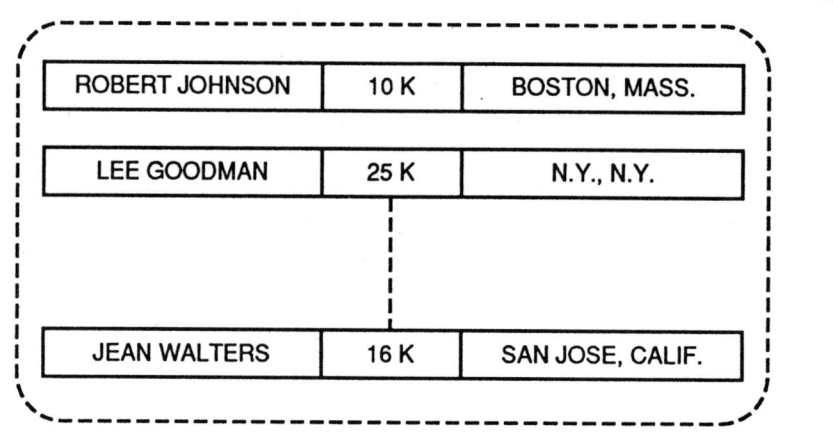

Figure 2. An EMPLOYEE file.

A *database* is a collection of records of different types (Figure 3). The records in a database are linked to each other so that relevant data items in different records can be retrieved without difficulty. For example, we may wish to link together all records of employees who work for the same department (see Figure 4), so that it is easy to find out who works for a particular department. Figure 4 illustrates the

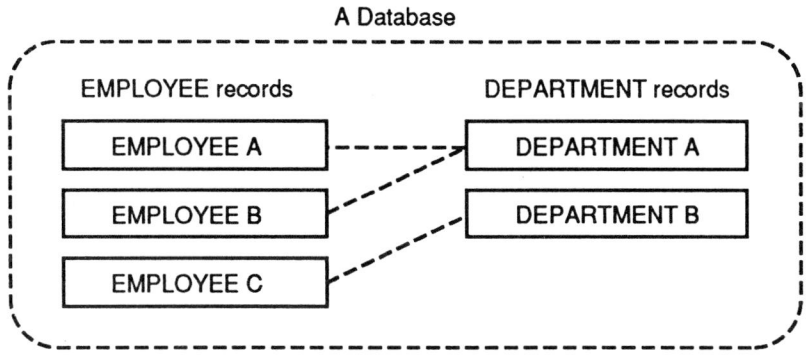

Figure 3. A database with two types of records.

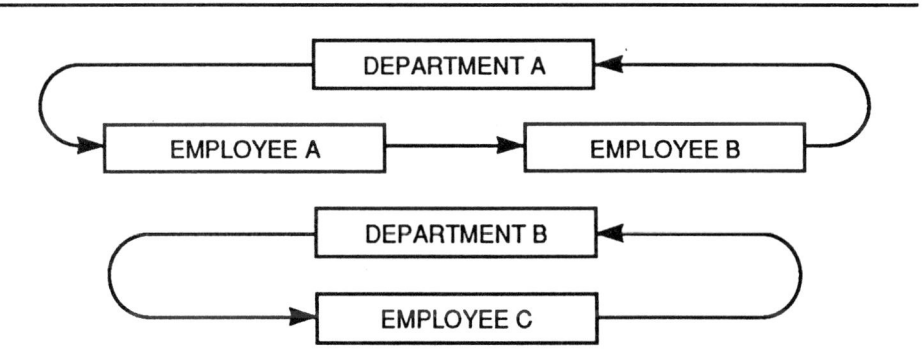

Figure 4. Relevant records in the database are linked together (physical data structure of the database).

physical data structure of the database in which the connections between DEPARTMENT records and EMPLOYEE records are implemented by chains. A DEPARTMENT record has a pointer which points to the first EMPLOYEE record in the chain. Each EMPLOYEE record in the chain has a pointer which points to the next EMPLOYEE record in the chain. The last EMPLOYEE record points back to the DEPARTMENT record. Figure 4 illustrates the relationships of record *occurrences* in the database, but it is too detailed to be useful to communicate the key relationships in the database. Figure 5 is a simple way to represent

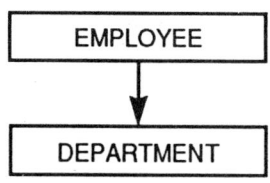

Figure 5. Logical data structure of the database.

the record organization in Figure 4. Each rectangular box in Figure 5 represents a record *type*, and the arrow represents the association of EMPLOYEE records with their DEPARTMENT records. There is another distinction between Figures 4 and 5; Figure 5 represents the *logical data structure* of the database since it shows only the connection between the DEPARTMENT record type and the EMPLOYEE record type, but it does not show how this connection is implemented.

1.2   LOGICAL DATABASE DESIGN AND PHYSICAL DATABASE DESIGN

Database design can be divided into two steps: logical design and physical design (see Figure 6).

"Physical database design" is the process of selecting a physical data structure for a given logical data structure. For example, there are at least three (3) possible physical data structures within a CODASYL database system to support the same logical data structure in Figure 6. The first is to use a "forward pointer" to link all the EMPLOYEE records in the same department. The second is to add "backward pointer" to the EMPLOYEE records. The third is to use "pointer array" in which the DEPARTMENT record maintains pointers to all related EMPLOYEE records. Each of these three physical data structures has its own advantages and disadvantages. The first one is easy to implement and is suitable for sequential processing of the EMPLOYEE records. The second one makes it relatively easy to find the previous EMPLOYEE records in the chain at the expense of more storage space needed by the backward pointers (it also makes the deletion process more efficient). The key advantage of the third physical data structure is that all EMPLOYEE records belonging to the same

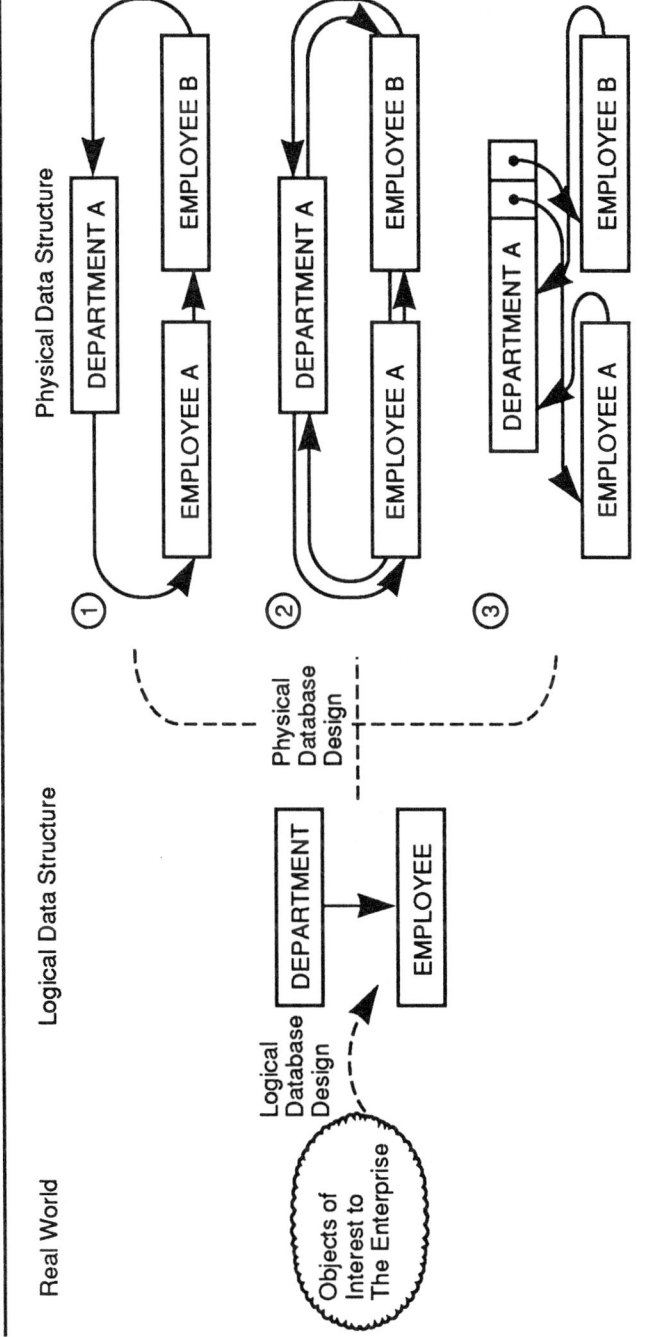

Figure 6. Logical and physical database design.

department can be retrieved at once. It is important to note that no physical data structure is universally optimal. The purpose of physical database design is to select the physical data structure which is most suitable for the given application environment. Although physical database design is an important topic, we shall not discuss it further in this monograph.

"Logical database design" is the process of designing the logical data structure for the database (see Figure 6). This involves an analysis of the application environment and the logical data structure types available in the database system. Currently, there are few tools to aid the logical database design process; the database designer usually has to rely on intuition and experience. As a result, many databases existing today are not properly designed.

In this monograph, we shall concentrate on the logical database design process and introduce a useful and practical tool to help the database designer.

1.3 DATABASE SYSTEMS AND DATA MODELS

There are many database systems in use at the moment. They can be classified into three (3) major categories: hierarchical, network and relational. One of the major differences among them is the type of logical data structures which can be supported. Hierarchical database systems, such as IBM's Information Management System (IMS), require data record types to be organized in a hierarchical form (see Figure 7). This hierarchical data structure works well with some databases but it becomes difficult to design databases using a hierarchical database system when a natural hierarchy among record types does not exist. Network (or CODASYL) database systems, such as Honeywell's Integrated Data Store (IDS), UNIVAC's DMS-1100, and Cullinane's IDMS, provide more complex data structure capabilities than the hierarchical database systems. For example, network database systems allow a record type to have multiple record types as its "parents" (see Figure 8). Relational systems (most of which are presently experimental) use tables as the logical data structures (see Figure 9).

In short, logical database design is concerned with organizing data into a form acceptable to the underlying database system (see Figure 10).

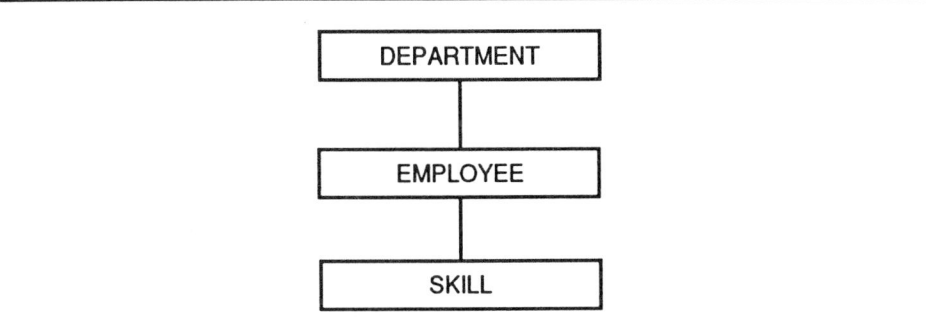

Figure 7. "Hierarchical" data structure.

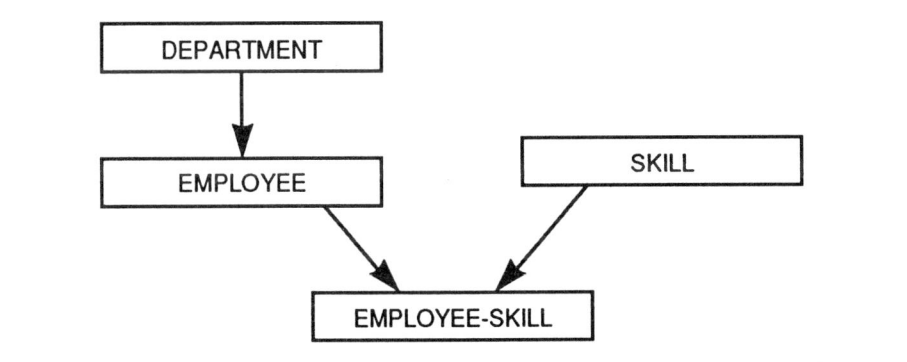

Figure 8. "Network" data structure.

1.4 PROBLEMS IN LOGICAL DATABASE DESIGN

Database design today is a complicated process since the database designer has to consider not only how to model the real world, but also the limitations of the database system and the efficiency of retrieval and updating. Examples are:

(1) The database designer is constrained by the limited data structure types supported by the database system. For example, the many-to-many relationships between two types of entities, such as the relationships between employees and projects, cannot be represented directly in many database systems.

8 THE ENTITY-RELATIONSHIP APPROACH TO LOGICAL DATABASE DESIGN

DEPARTMENT TABLE

D#	BUDGET
1	10 M
5	5 M
8	20 M
.	.
.	.
.	.

EMPLOYEE TABLE

NAME	SALARY	ADDRESS
JOHNSON	10 K	BOSTON
GOODMAN	15 K	NYC
WALTERS	16 K	SAN JOSE
.	.	.
.	.	.
.	.	.

SKILL TABLE

S#	S-NAME
5	FORTRAN
2	COBOL
1	PL/I
.	.
.	.
.	.

EMPLOYEE-SKILL TABLE

NAME	S#
JOHNSON	1
JOHNSON	2
GOODMAN	1
GOODMAN	5
.	.
.	.
.	.

DEPARTMENT-EMPLOYEE TABLE

D#	NAME
1	JOHNSON
1	GOODMAN
5	WALTERS
.	.
.	.
.	.

Figure 9. "Relational" ("table") data structure.

(2) The database designer may have to consider the access path of the records (i.e., how to access a particular record type). For instance, the implicit assumption in Figure 3 is that EMPLOYEE records have to be accessed via the corresponding DEPARTMENT record.

(3) The database designer may want to consider how to make the retrieval and updating more efficient. Thus, the data about an entity in the real world may be put into more than one record for efficiency purposes. For instance, the data

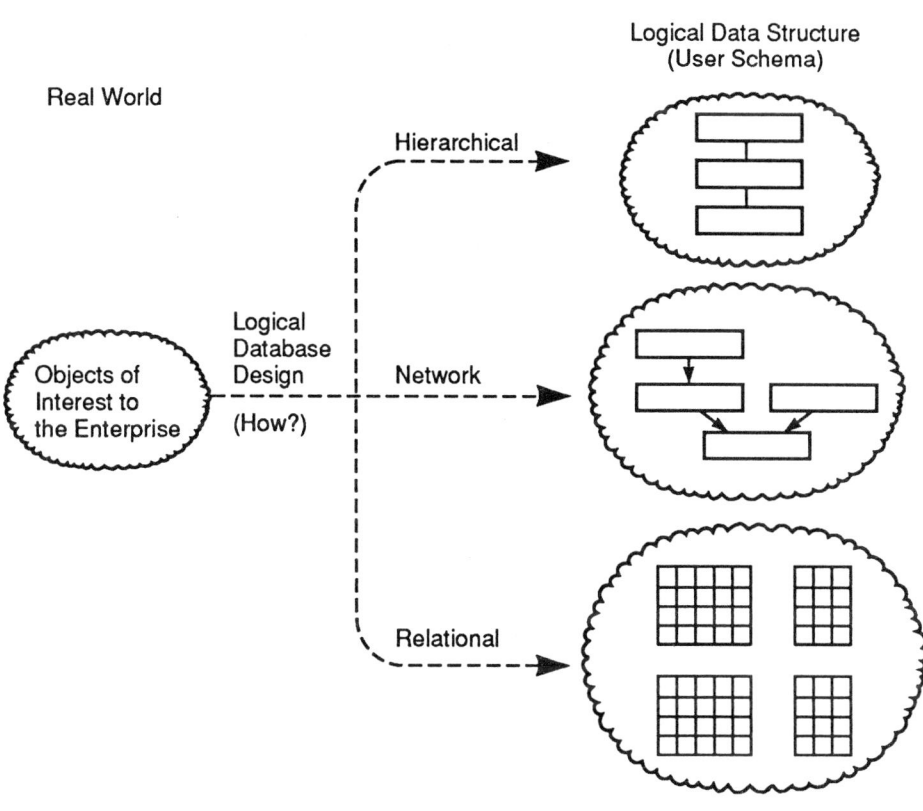

Figure 10. Logical database design.

items about an employee may be grouped in two records: EMPLOYEE-MASTER and EMPLOYEE-DETAIL.

There are two problems in the conventional database design approach:

(1) The database designer has to consider many issues at the same time, which makes the database design task very difficult.

(2) The final output of the logical database design process is the user schema (i.e., a description of the user view of database). Since the user schema represents the database designer's solution to the complicated issues mentioned

above, it is not difficult to see why user schemata are usually difficult to understand and difficult to change.

1.5 A NEW APPROACH TO DATABASE DESIGN: THE ENTITY-RELATIONSHIP APPROACH

We shall describe a new approach to logical database design called the *Entity-Relationship (E-R) approach*. The key idea of the E-R approach is to add an intermediate stage in logical database design (see Figure 11). The database designer first identifies the entities and relationships which are of interest to the enterprise using the *Entity-Relationship (E-R) diagrammatic technique*. At this stage, the database designer should view the data from the point of view of the whole enterprise (not the view of a particular application programmer). Therefore, we shall call the description of the *enterprise view* of data the "enterprise schema". The enterprise schema should be "pure" representation of the real world and should be independent of storage and efficiency considerations. The database designer first designs the enterprise schema and then translates it to a user schema for his database system (see Figure 11).

1.6 ADVANTAGES OF THE ENTITY-RELATIONSHIP APPROACH

The conventional approaches to logical database design usually have only one phase: mapping the information about objects in the real world directly to a user schema. The E-R approach to logical database design consists of two major phases: (1) defining the enterprise schema using the entity-relationship diagram, and (2) translating the enterprise schema into a user schema. The advantages of the E-R approach are:

(1) The division of functionalities and labor into two phases makes the database design process simpler and better organized.

(2) The enterprise schema is easier to design than the user schema since it need not be restricted by the capabilities of the database system, and is independent of the storage and efficiency considerations.

(3) The enterprise schema is more stable than the user schema.

INTRODUCTION   11

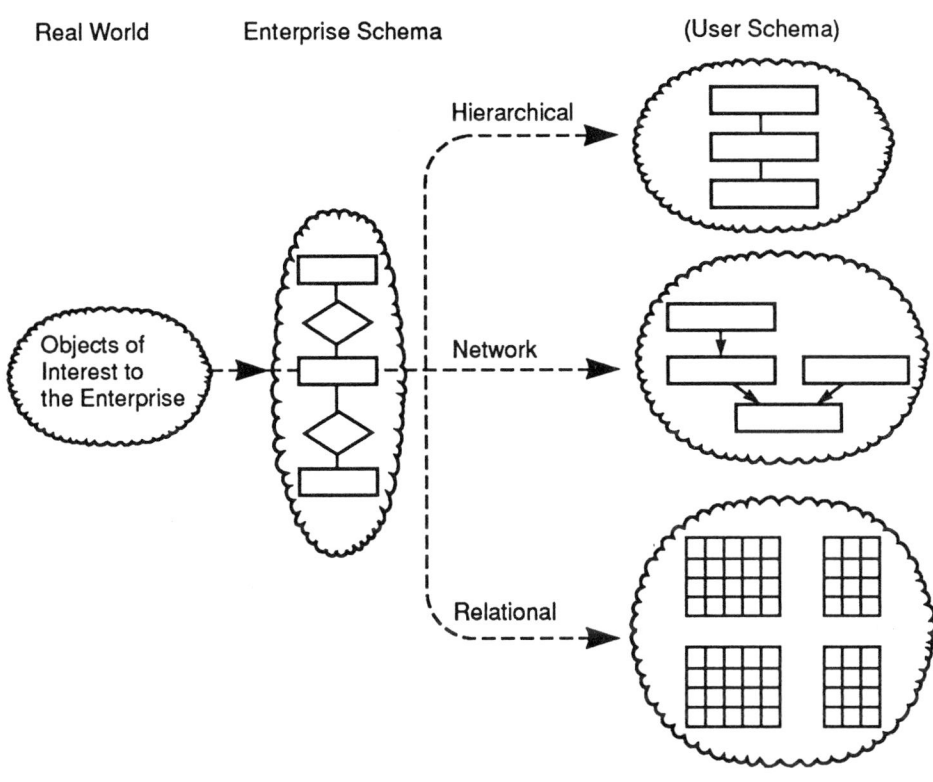

Figure 11.   Enterprise schema – an intermediate step in logical database design.

If one wants to change from one database system to another, one would probably have to change the user schema but not the enterprise schema, since the enterprise schema is independent of the database systems used. What needs to be done is to remap the enterprise schema to a user schema suitable for the new database system. Similarly, if one wants to change the user schema to optimize a new application program, one need not change the enterprise schema, but rather remap the enterprise schema to a new user schema.

(4) The enterprise schema expressed by the entity-relationship diagram is more easily understood by non-EDP people.

E-R Approach and ANSI/X3/SPARC Proposal   2

2.1 ANSI/X3/SPARC PROPOSAL

The concept of the enterprise schema is very similar to the concept of conceptual schema proposed by the ANSI/X3/SPARC group. In this section, we shall discuss the ANSI/X3/SPARC architecture and how to apply the E-R approach to this architecture.

In the fall of 1971, the Committee on Computer and Information Processing (abbreviated as X3 Committee) of the American National Standards Institute (ANSI) formed a special study group to determine which (if any) aspects of database management systems are suitable candidates for the development of standards. The special study group, which is called the Standards Planning and Requirements Committee (SPARC), consists of representatives from the user community, hardware manufacturers, and universities.

The ANSI/X3/SPARC group spent considerable time and effort considering different views of database theory and developing a vocabulary that was consistent and mutually comprehensible. As a result, their interim report has attracted considerable attention in the database community.

What the ANSI/X3/SPARC group learned was that it is not desirable to develop standards that specify how components of a database management system are to work, but rather to focus on how components are meshed together (i.e., the interfaces). With this in mind, the interim report outlines a three schema architecture of a database management system (see Figure 12). Current database management systems usually have a two level structure: the logical structure (i.e., the structure of data as seen by the programmer) and the physical structure (i.e., the structure of data as seen by the computer).

The ANSI/X3/SPARC proposal has a three level structure: external schema, conceptual schema and internal schema (see Figure 12). The external schema (user schema) represents the user's (i.e., programmer's) view of data. In other words, an *external schema* is a description of data visible to an application program in terms of names and characteristics of data. The *internal schema* represents the physical data organization in the storage devices. It also contains the details of integrity, recovery, and efficient ways of retrieving and updating data. The *conceptual* schema represents the enterprise view of data. It is a description of a model of the enterprise in terms of its entities, attributes, and the relationships among them. It also contains the requirements for permitted operations, semantic integrity and privacy. The conceptual schema is intended to provide a stable view of data.

2.2 CONCEPTUAL SCHEMA AND ENTERPRISE SCHEMA

What is the difference between the conceptual schema proposed by ANSI/X3/SPARC group and the enterprise schema discussed in this monograph? The answer is that they are almost the same except that the conceptual schema is required to serve as the interface between the external schema and the internal schema (see Figure 12).

One reason for using the conceptual schema as the interface is to reduce the number of mappings between the external schemata and the internal schemata. For example, if there are M external schemata and N internal schemata, we need M•N programs to do the mappings between the external schemata and the internal schemata (Figure 13). If there is a conceptual schema between the external schemata and the internal schemata, we need only M+N programs to do the mappings (Figure 14). Therefore, the number of mapping programs is reduced dramatically.

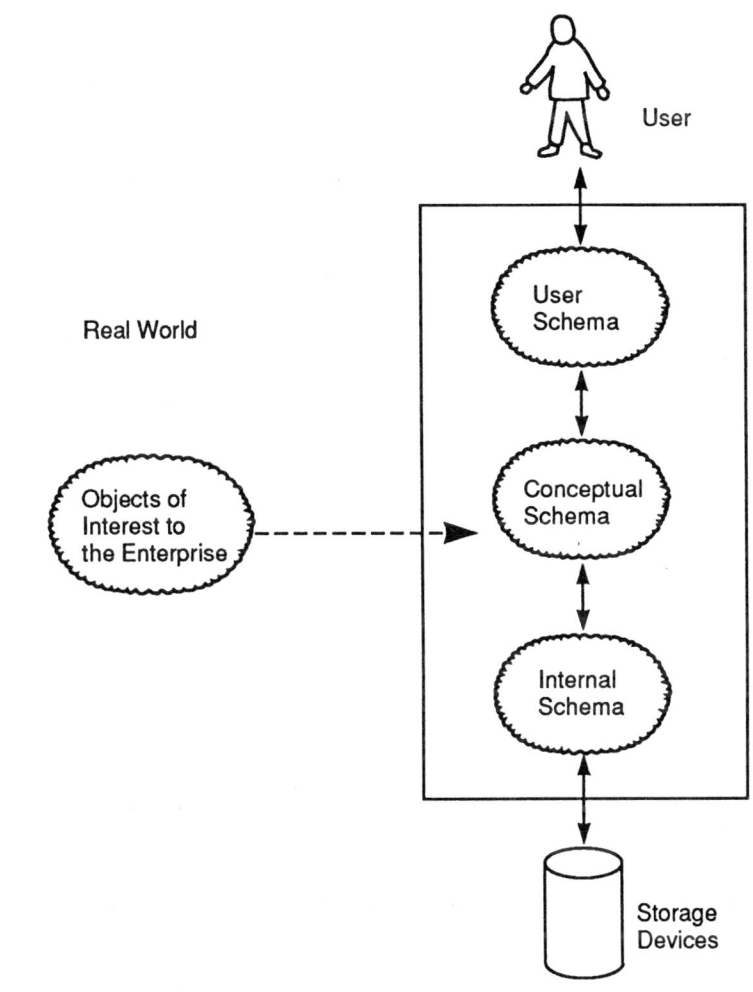

Figure 12. ANSI/X3/SPARC architecture.

One of the goals of the ANSI/X3/SPARC architecture is to keep conceptual schema relatively stable while allowing changes in external schemata and internal schemata. This goal does not seem difficult to achieve since the conceptual schema represents the enterprise view of data and should be relatively stable compared with the user view of

16 THE ENTITY-RELATIONSHIP APPROACH TO LOGICAL DATABASE DESIGN

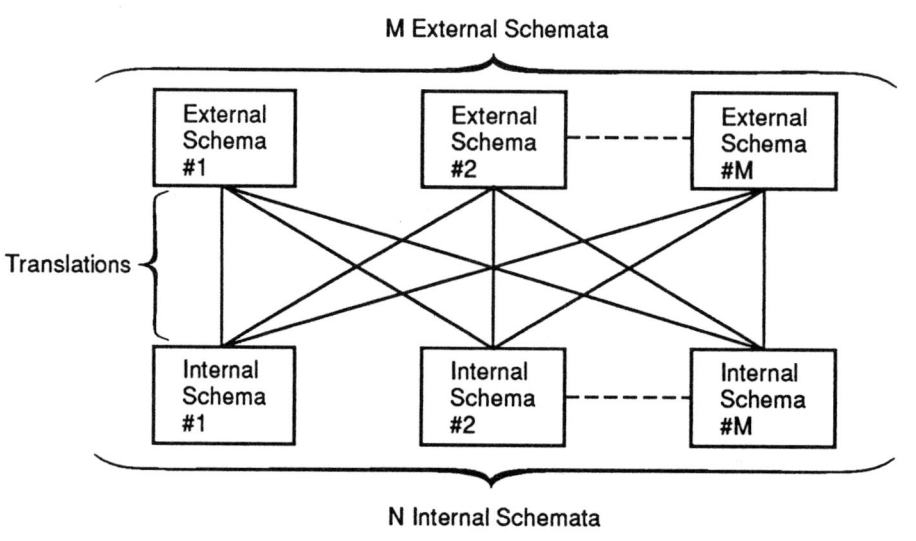

Figure 13. Translation between external schemata and internal schemata without a conceptual schema.

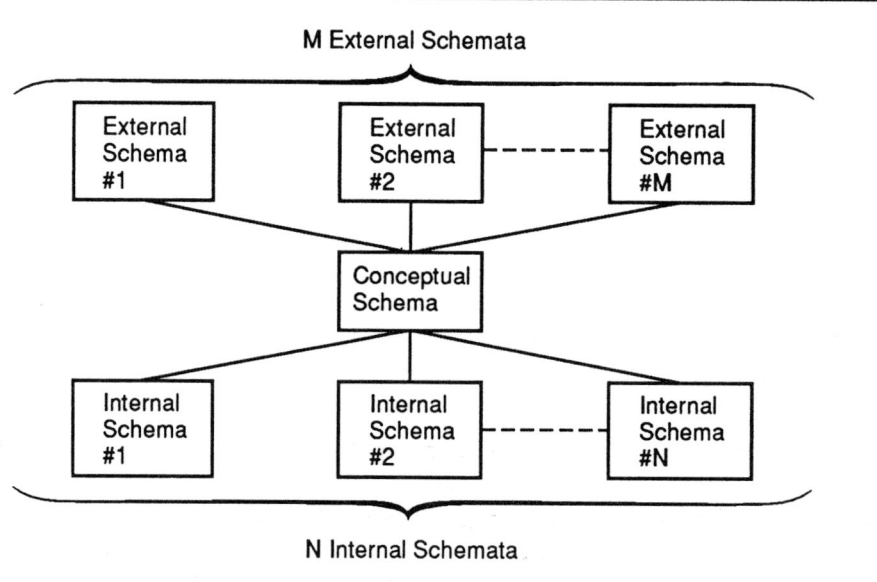

Figure 14. Using conceptual schema as the interface between external.

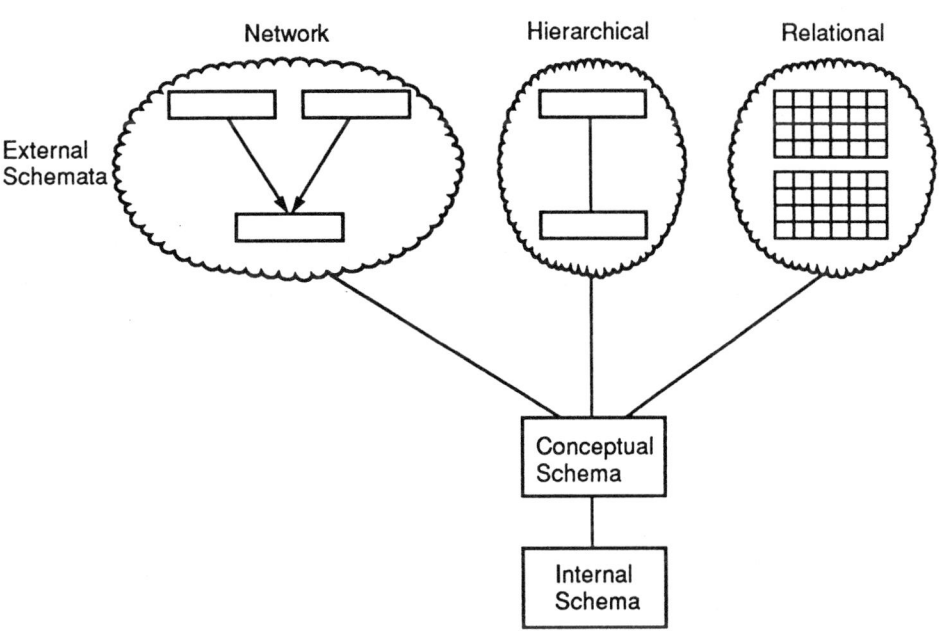

Figure 15. External schemata may be expressed in different data-structure types.

physical view of data. Therefore, when physical database organization is changed or data is moved from "old-type" storage devices to "new-type" storage devices, we only change the internal schema, and not the conceptual schema or external schemata. Similarly, if a user wants to view data as a certain kind of organization, we may design an external schema for him without changing the conceptual schema and the internal schemata.

Besides serving as an interface between external schemata and internal schemata, the conceptual schema is the same as the enterprise schema, and we can use the entity-relationship diagram to describe the conceptual schema. In addition, since the external schemata may be expressed in terms of different data-structure types such as network (CODASYL), hierarchical, or relational (see Figure 15), the translation rules between E-R diagrams and different data-structure types discussed later in this monograph would be very useful in the implementation of ANSI/X3/SPARC architecture.

2.3 THREE TYPES OF ADMINISTRATORS OF DATABASES

The ANSI/X3/SPARC group has identified three types of database administrators:

(1) *Enterprise Administrator*

The enterprise administrator defines the *conceptual schema* and, if possible, validates it. He must understand very well both the operations of the enterprise and the meaning of its information (data). He is responsible for the content, integrity and security of the database.

(2) *Database Administrator*

The database administrator defines the *internal schema*. He designs the physical data structures, coding schemes, access paths, and placement of data in storage devices. He is responsible for the efficient utilization of the storage space as well as the performance of the database system.

(3) *Application Administrator*

An external schema represents an application programmer's view of data. It is envisioned that each general application area will have its own application administrator who provides the external schemata for that area. But these external schemata have to be consistent and derivable from a single conceptual schema. Note that the same external schemata can be used by several application programmers, not necessarily working on the same program.

These three types of administrators represent three different roles which may be played by an individual or a group of people. Although the distinctions among these three types of administrators of database are clear in terms of ANSI/X3/SPARC's three schema architecture, it is not clear in conventional database environments. As a matter of fact, the "database administrator" as defined today in many organizations, has all the responsibilities of the above-mentioned three types of administrators. In terms of the scope of this monograph, we are primarily concerned with the responsibility of the enterprise administrator (i.e., the task of modeling the real world) and the responsibility of the application administrator (i.e., the task of designing the external schemata).

2.4 RELEVANCE TO THE E-R APPROACH

In summary, should the ANSI/X3/SPARC architecture become reality, the E-R approach can be used in the following ways:

(1) In the design of conceptual schema.

(2) In the translation of conceptual schema to external schemata.

Entity-Relationship (E-R) Diagram

3

In this chapter we shall introduce the entity-relationship diagrammatic technique. We shall first discuss what entities and relationships are, and then explain how to describe properties of entities and relationships.

3.1 ENTITIES AND RELATIONSHIPS

3.1.1 Entity Type

An entity is a "thing" which can be distinctly identified. Entities can be classified into different entity types, such as EMPLOYEE and STOCKHOLDER (See Figure 16). In the E-R diagram, an entity type is represented by a rectangular-shaped box (see Figure 17).

There are many "things" in the real world. Some of them are of interest to the enterprise, and the rest are not. It is the responsibility of the database designer to select the entity types which are most suitable for his/her company.

3.1.2 Relationship Type

Relationships may exist between entities. For example, MARRIAGE is a relationship between two person entities (see Figure 18). Relationships can be classified into different *relationship types*. For instance, PROJ-EMP and PROJ-MANAGER are two different relationship types between

22 THE ENTITY-RELATIONSHIP APPROACH TO LOGICAL DATABASE DESIGN

Figure 16. Entities and entity types.

EMPLOYEE   STOCK-HOLDER

Figure 17. Entity types are represented by rectangular-shaped box.

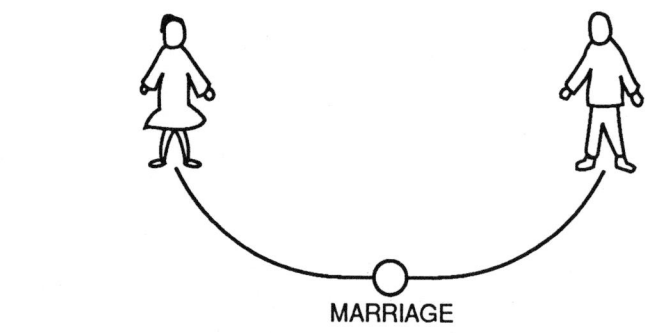

Figure 18. MARRIAGE as a relationship between two person entities.

two entity types, PROJ (project) and EMP (employee). In entity-relationship diagrammatic notation, a relationship type is represented by a diamond-shaped box with lines connected to related entity types (see Figure 19). The "m" and "1" notion associated with the relationship type PROJ-MANAGER in Figure 16 indicates that each project has only one manager, but that an employee can be the manager of many projects. The "m" and "n" associated with the relationship type PROJ-EMP indicates that it is a many-to-many mapping. That is, each project may consist of several employees, and each employee may be associated with more than on project. Note that other types of mapping between entities are also possible. For instance, the relationship type MARRIAGE is a one-to-one mapping between person entities (Figure 20).

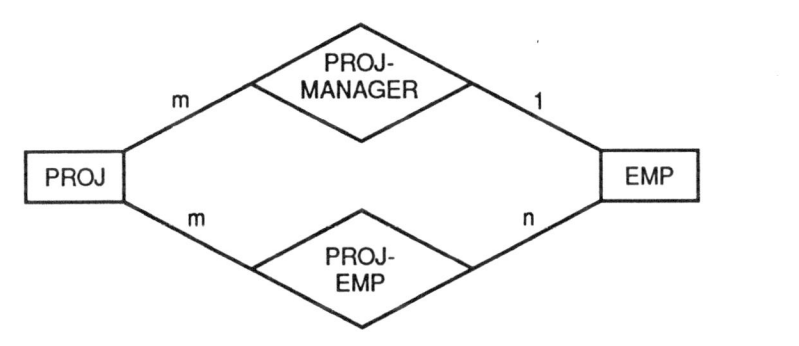

Figure 19. Relationship types are represented by diamond-shaped box.

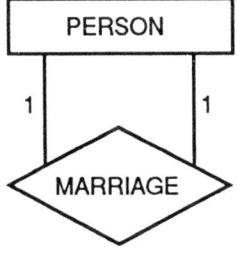

Figure 20. MARRIAGE as a relationship type between PERSON entities.

24 THE ENTITY-RELATIONSHIP APPROACH TO LOGICAL DATABASE DESIGN

It is possible to define a relationship type among more than two entity types. For example, PART-SUPP-PROJ, which describes what parts are supplied by particular suppliers to particular projects (Figure 21), is a relationship type defined on three entity types: PART, SUPP (supplier), and PROJ (Figure 22).

Note that a 3-way relationship usually cannot be replaced by three binary relationships. As an example, the 3-way relationship PART-SUPP-PROJ in Figure 21 is replaced by three binary relationships: PART-SUPP, SUPP-PROJ, and PROJ-PART (see Figure 23). However, if we want to construct the 3-way relationship starting with these three binary relationships, we get some "non-facts" (see the starred entries in Figure 24).

There are many types of relationships between entities, and some of them are of interest to the enterprise; the database designer is responsible for the selection of the relationship types relevant to the enterprise. He should also specify the types of mapping of the relationship types (e.g., one-to-one, one-to-many, many-to-many).

PART #	SUPPLIER #	PROJ #
25	4	1
25	5	2
10	4	2
10	4	3
17	2	1
17	5	1

Figure 21. Information about PART-SUPP-PROJ relationships.

ENTITY-RELATIONSHIP (E-R) DIAGRAM   25

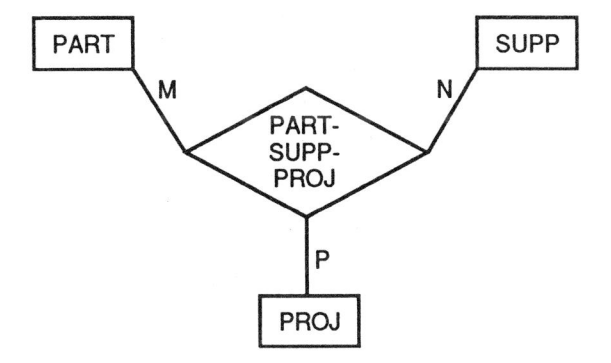

Figure 22. PART-SUPP-PROJ as a relationship type.

PART #	SUPP #
25	4
25	5
10	4
17	2
17	5

SUPP #	PROJ #
4	1
4	2
4	3
5	1
5	2
2	1

PROJ #	PART #
1	25
1	17
2	10
2	25
3	10

Figure 23. Information about three binary relationships: PART-SUPP, SUPP-PROJ, and PROJ-PART.

26 THE ENTITY-RELATIONSHIP APPROACH TO LOGICAL DATABASE DESIGN

SUPP #	SUPP #	PROJ #
25	4	1
25	4	2
25	5	1
25	5	2
10	4	2
10	4	3
17	2	1
17	5	1

Figure 24. Information generated from three binary relationships in Figure 23.

3.2 DESCRIPTIONS OF ENTITIES AND RELATIONSHIPS

3.2.1 Attributes and Values

Entities and relationships have properties, which can be expressed in terms of attribute-value pairs. For example, in the statement "the AGE OF EMPLOYEE x is 24", "AGE" is an "attribute" of employee x, and "24" is the "value" of the attribute AGE. Values can be classified into different *value types* such as NO-OF-YEARS, QUANTITY, and COLOR. In the E-R diagrammatic notation, a value type is represented by a circle (see Figure 25) and an attribute is represented by an arrow directed from the entity type to the desired value type.

In some cases, an attribute may have more than one value for a given entity. For instance, "PHONE-NO" of employee x may have two values: 253-6606 and 253-9999. In this case, we put "1:n" in the arrow to indicate that it is a multi-valued attribute. This is similar to the "repeating group" concept in conventional data processing. However, many attributes, such as "AGE" and "SOC-SEC-NO", are single-valued. For simplicity, we do not associate anything such as "1:1" with the arrows in the E-R diagram for such attributes.

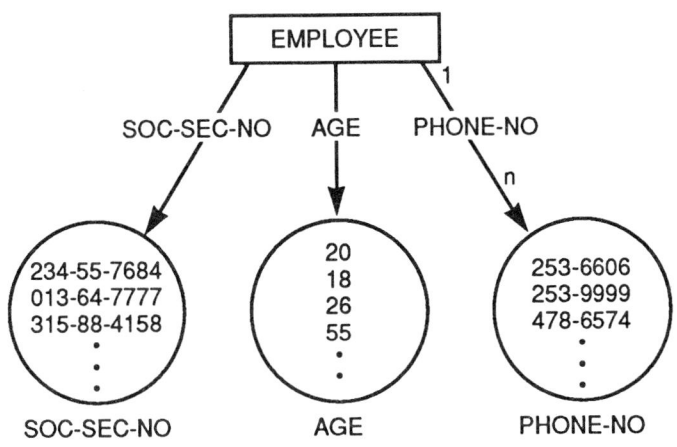

Figure 25. Value types and attributes.

So far we have considered only the attributes of entities. Sometimes we are also interested in the properties of a relationship. For instance, we may want to know when employee x started working on a particular project. The STARTING-DATE is neither an attribute of EMPLOYEE nor an attribute of PROJ since its value depends on both the particular employee and the project involved. Therefore, STARTING-DATE is an attribute of the relationship PROJ-EMP. Another example of "attribute of relationship" is PERCENTAGE-OF-EFFORT, which is the percentage of time that an employee devotes to a particular project (see Figure 26). The concept of "attribute of relationship" is important in understanding the semantics of data. The concept is similar to the "relationship data" in "network" (CODASYL) type database systems, and similar to the "intersection data" in hierarchical-type (IMS-type) database systems.

3.2.2 Entity Identifier

The entities discussed so far are those which exist in our minds or can be identified by pointing our finger at them. When someone asks, "What color is it?", "it" is either understood by both the speaker and the listener or is identified by pointing a finger to the subject. This identification scheme can work for very few objects, and we will run into

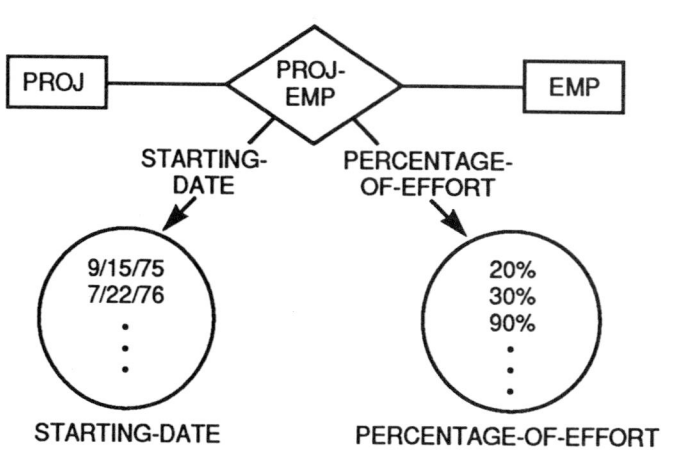

Figure 26. Attributes of relationship.

difficulties when we want to communicate the information about a variety of objects to many different people. Therefore, in both daily conversation and computer data processing, we need another scheme to identify entities. A commonly used scheme is the use of attribute-value pairs to identify entities. Every entity has many attributes, but which one should be chosen? The answer is that the attributes chosen should be able to absolutely identify the entities. For instance, we may use the attribute NAME to identify employees in a small company, but not in a large company. These chosen attributes of the entity are called the *entity identifiers*. In some cases, it may be difficult or inconvenient to use available attributes as the entity identifier. What we may do is to create an artificial attribute which can positively identify the entities. Examples are "SOC-SEC-NO", "EMP-NO", "PART-NO", and "PROJ-NO". The concept of "entity identifier" is similar to the concept of "primary key" in conventional data processing.

3.2.3 Relationship Identifier

Relationships are identified by utilizing the identifiers of the entities involved in the relationship. For example, if a project is identified by its PROJ-NO and an employee is identified by EMP-NO, then the PROJ-EMP relationship is identified by *both* PROJ-NO and EMP-NO. In some situations, a relationship type is defined between two occurrences of the same entity type. For instance, MARRIAGE is a relationship type defined between occurrences of the same entity type, PERSON. In order to positively identify such relationships, we not only use the entity identifier, but also indicate what role the entity plays in the relationship. In the case of MARRIAGE, we shall attach the role names HUSBAND and WIFE to the entity identifier NAME, where HUSBAND and WIFE are the "roles" they play in the relationship MARRIAGE.

3.3 SPECIAL ENTITY AND RELATIONSHIP TYPES

In this section, we shall discuss several special entity types and relationship types which are commonly encountered.

3.3.1 Existence Dependency

The existence of an entity may depend on the existence of another entity type. For example, the existence of CHILDREN entities in the database depends on the existence of the associated employees. In other words, if an employee leaves the company, we shall not keep track of his children. Figure 27 illustrates the E-R diagram for this situation. CHILDREN is represented by a double-rectangular-shaped box, which means that it is a "weak" entity type. The existence of a weak entity depends on the existence of other entities. The "E" inside the relationship box indicates that it is an "existence dependent" relationship; the arrow associated with the relationship box indicates the direction of the dependency.

It is possible that the "existence dependent" relationship is a many-to-many mapping. For example, if the father leaves the company, the CHILDREN entities may still exist if their mother is still an employee of the company. This situation is represented in the E-R diagram shown in Figure 28.

3.3.2 ID Dependency

If an entity cannot be uniquely identified by its own attributes and has to be identified by its relationships with other entities, it has "ID dependency" on other entities. For example, "street" is only unique

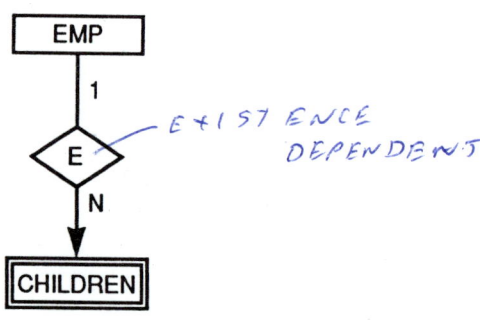

Figure 27. An existence dependent relationship type and a weak entity type.

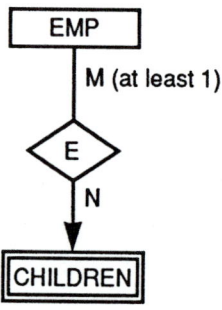

Figure 28. An "existence dependent" relationship may also be a many-to-many mapping.

within a city, a city is only unique within a state, and a state is only unique within a country. In order to uniquely identify the address of a location, we have to specify the names of the city, state, and country in addition to the name of the street. The "ID Dependency" is indicated by the "ID" in the relationship box, and the direction of the relationship is indicated by the arrow (see Figure 29); most ID dependencies are

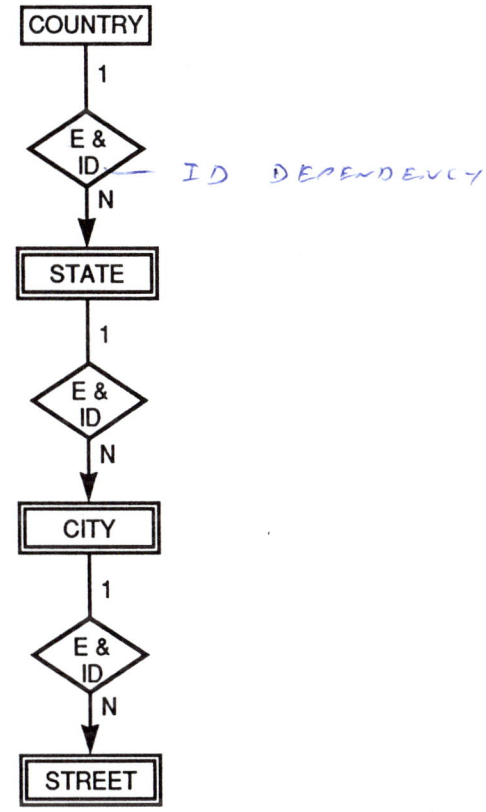

Figure 29. "Existence dependency" and "ID dependency".

associated with existence dependencies. However, existence dependency does not imply ID dependency. For example, the CHILDREN entities in Figure 30 are identified with their own attribute(s) and their parent(s)' ID (see Figure 31), while the CHILDREN entities in Figure 27 may be identified by their own CHILDREN-NO (see Figure 32).

32 THE ENTITY-RELATIONSHIP APPROACH TO LOGICAL DATABASE DESIGN

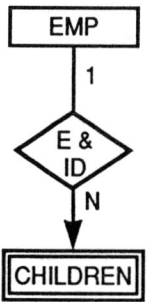

Figure 30. "Existence dependency" and "ID dependency".

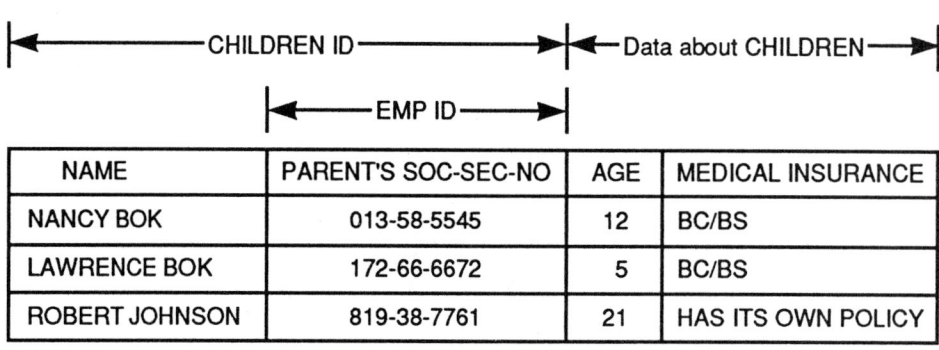

Figure 31. "ID dependency".

CHILDREN-NO	NAME	AGE	MEDICAL INSURANCE
1011	NANCY BOK	12	BC/BS
1025	LAWRENCE BOK	5	BC/BS
1044	ROBERT JOHNSON	21	HAS ITS OWN POLICY

(CHILDREN-NO is CHILDREN ID)

Figure 32. No "ID dependency".

Translation of E-R Diagrams into Data-Structure Diagrams 4

4.1 DATA-STRUCTURE DIAGRAMS

The logical data structures of databases supported by Codasyl (network) type database system can be expressed in terms of data-structure diagrams. Figure 33 illustrates a data-structure diagram. Each rectangular box represents a record type, such as EMP and DEPENDENT. The arrow represents a data-structure set, which connects two record types together. The record type in which the arrow originates is the *owner record type* of the data-structure set, and the record type in which the arrow ends is the *member record type* of the data-structure set. In Figure 33, EMP is the owner record type, and DEPENDENT is the member record type. In a data-structure set, the owner record may have zero, one, or more member records (occurrences). A member record in a data-structure set has exactly one owner record. In our example, each employee record may be connected to many DEPENDENT records, or to none. However, each DEPENDENT record must be associated with exactly one EMP record. This is illustrated in Figure 34. Conceptually, the arrow represents a 1:n (one-to-many) association between the owner record type and the member record type. This kind of association can also be represented in table form (Figure 35).

Figure 36 illustrates a more complicated data structure. The EMPLOYEE record type is the owner record type of a data-structure set in which the EMPLOYEE-SKILL is the member record type. The record type EMPLOYEE-SKILL is also the member record type of

34 THE ENTITY-RELATIONSHIP APPROACH TO LOGICAL DATABASE DESIGN

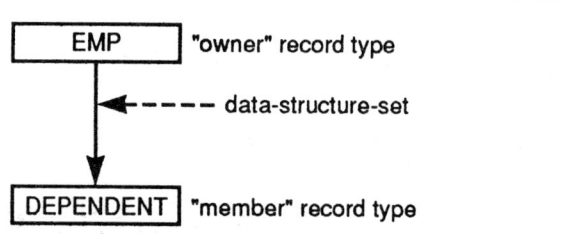

Figure 33. A data-structure diagram.

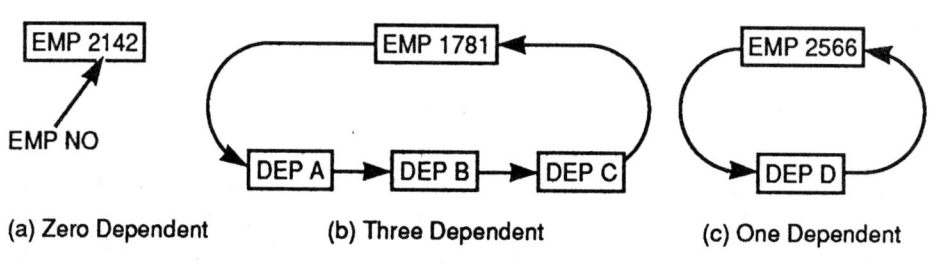

(a) Zero Dependent   (b) Three Dependent   (c) One Dependent

Figure 34. An "owner" record may have zero, one, or more "member" records.

EMP-NO	DEPENDENT
1781	A
1781	B
1781	C
2566	D
⋮	⋮

Figure 35. One-to-many correspondence between employee and dependents.

another data-structure set in which the SKILL record type is the owner record. Actually, the EMPLOYEE-SKILL record contains the cross-reference information about EMPLOYEES and SKILLS. This kind of information can be represented in table form as shown in Figure 37.

We can see from Figure 37 that an employee may have one or more skills and that usually more than one employee has a particular skill. Therefore, the relationship between employees and skills is m:n (many-to-many). This m:n correspondence between employees and skills can be derived from Figure 36. The data-structure sets in Figure 36 show that there exists a 1:m (one-to-many) mapping between EMPLOYEE record type and EMPLOYEE-SKILL record type, and that a similar mapping (1:n) exists between SKILL record type and the EMP-

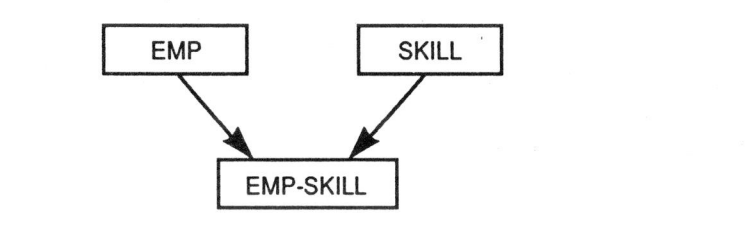

Figure 36. Two data-structure-sets have the same "member" record type.

EMP-NO	SKILL
2142	COBOL
2142	PL/1
1781	COBOL
2566	PL/1
⋮	⋮

Figure 37. Cross-reference information about EMPLOYEES and SKILLS.

36 THE ENTITY-RELATIONSHIP APPROACH TO LOGICAL DATABASE DESIGN

SKILL record type. Therefore, the correspondence between the EMP record and the skill record type is m:n (many-to-many).

The data-structure diagram in Figure 36 can be implemented using a pointer array as shown in Figure 38. The data-structure set between EMP record type and SKILL record type is represented by the solid lines, and the data-structure set between the SKILL record type and the EMP-SKILL record type is represented by dotted lines.

In Figure 38, how do we determine the skills of a particular employee? The first step is to locate the EMP record with EMP-NO = 2142 using a hashing algorithm or some other method. The second step is to find the first EMP-SKILL record related to this employee. Via the pointer shown by the dotted line, we can find a skill record with SKILL-NAME = COBOL. We then find the second EMPLOYEE-SKILL record related to the same employee record (via solid line pointers). From the EMP-SKILL record, we can go through the dotted line pointer to locate a SKILL record with SKILL-NAME = PL/1. We cannot then find anymore EMP-SKILL records related to the same EMPLOYEE records (i.e., we have found the information we require: the employee with EMP-NO = 2142 has two skills: COBOL and PL/1).

How do we find all the employees with a particular skill, say COBOL? First, we locate the SKILL record with SKILL-NAME =

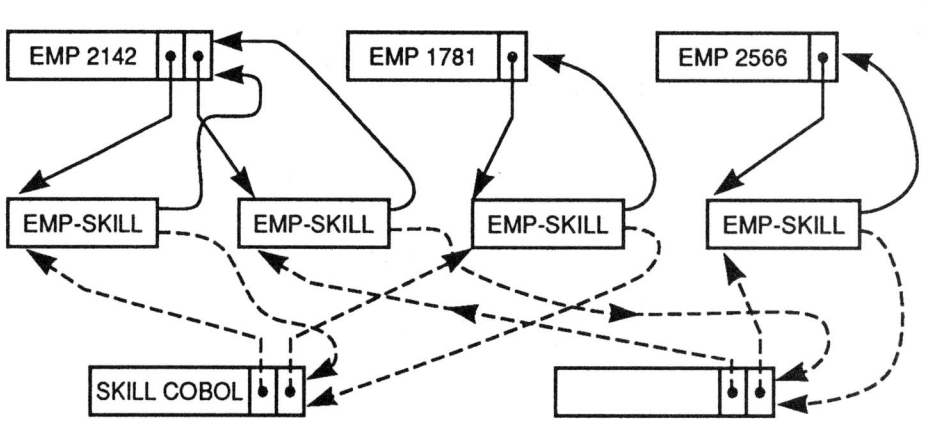

Figure 38. Implementation of the data-structure-sets in Figure 37 as "pointer arrays."

COBOL. Then we retrieve all EMP-SKILL records related to the SKILL record. For each EMPLOYEE-SKILL record, we retrieve, via the solid line pointer, the corresponding EMP record. By doing this, we know that there are two employees having the skill COBOL, and their employee numbers are 2142 and 1781.

Another way to implement the data-structure diagram in Figure 22 is to use "chains" as shown in Figure 39. The solid lines connect all the EMP-SKILL records related to the same EMP record. The dotted lines connect all the EMP-SKILL records related to the same SKILL record. Let us see how to find the skills of the employee with EMP-NO = 2142. We first find the first EMP-SKILL record via the solid line chain. From the EMP-SKILL record, we find the skill record via the dotted line chain. From the EMP-SKILL record, we search for the next EMP-SKILL record via the solid line chain. From the second EMP-SKILL record, we can determine the corresponding SKILL record through the dotted line chain. From the second EMP-SKILL record, we can find no more EMP-SKILL records in the solid line chain. Now, we know all the skills that employee 2142 has. Similarly, we can find all the employees with a certain skill by going through the chains.

Another type of data structure, which can usually be found in manufacturing databases, is shown in Figure 40. There are two record

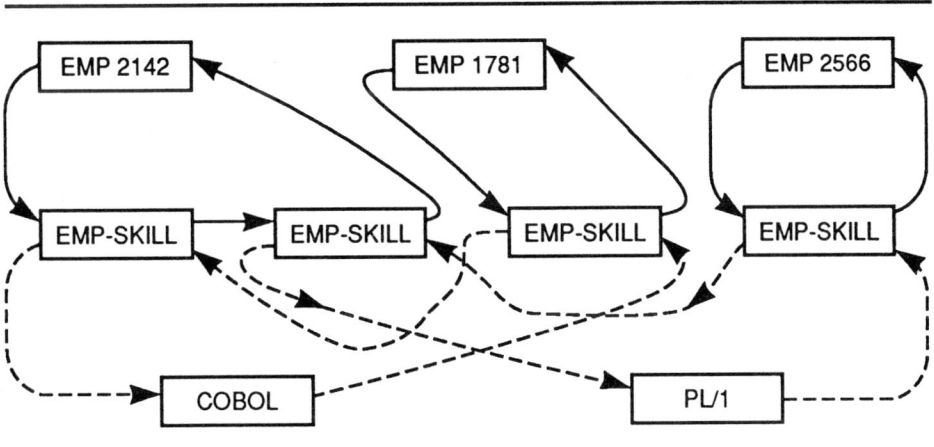

Figure 39. Implementation of the data-structure-sets in Figure 22 as "chains."

38 THE ENTITY-RELATIONSHIP APPROACH TO LOGICAL DATABASE DESIGN

types: PART and MFG-REL (manufacturing-relationship). Each product to be manufactured consists of many "parts" (components). Each part is, in turn, made of other parts. The PART record type contains information about the particular "part". The MFG-REL record type contains the information about the relationship between parts. Figure 41 illustrates this kind of relationship. It indicates that, in order to manufacture PART #1, we need five PART #2's and two PART #3's. We can also see that PART #3 is a sub-part of both PART #1 and PART #4. There are two data-structure sets in Figure 40, and they can be implemented as "chains" as shown in Figure 42. The solid lines represent the COMPONENT chain and the dotted lines represent the WHERE-USED chain. In order to find out the components of a particular part, we first retrieve all the MFG-REL records via the COMPONENT chain and, then, retrieve the corresponding subparts via the WHERE-USED chain. By doing this, we can find out that PART #4 consists of one PART #3 and two PART #5's. In order to find out where a particular part is used to manufacture other parts, we first retrieve all the MFG-REL records related to that particular PART record via the WHERE-USED chain, and then retrieve the corresponding PART records via the COMPONENT chain. By doing this, we can find out that two PART #5's are used in the manufacturing of PART #4.

Figures 33, 36 and 40 are the basic types of data-structure diagrams. A database can be expressed in a large data-structure diagram based on these three basic building blocks.

4.2 TRANSLATION RULES

As we have seen from the previous section, the data-structure diagram is closer to the physical organization of the database than the entity-relationship diagram. It is usually difficult to draw a data-structure diagram for the entities and relationships which are of interest to the enterprise. Therefore, we propose that the database designer first draw an E-R diagram to represent the enterprise view of data and then translate it to a data-structure diagram. In this section, we shall discuss how to translate an E-R diagram to a data-structure diagram. We identify several basic rules for translation based on the type of relationships between entities. We start with relationships defined by two entity types, then relationships defined by more than two entity

TRANSLATION OF E-R DIAGRAMS INTO DATA-STRUCTURE DIAGRAMS 39

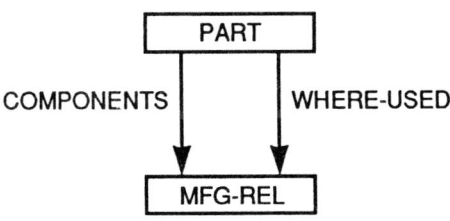

Figure 40. Two data-structure-sets have the same "owner" and "member" record types.

SUPER-PART-NO	SUB-PART-NO	QTY
1	2	5
1	3	2
4	3	1
4	5	2

Figure 41. Manufacturing relationship between parts.

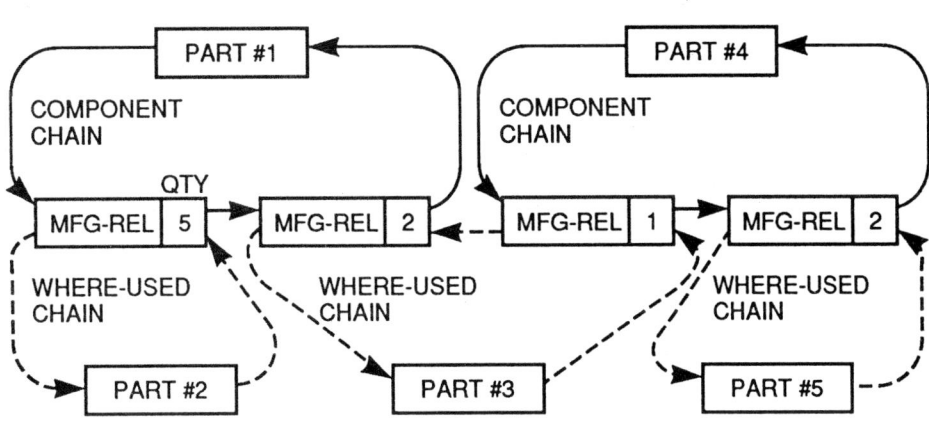

Figure 42. Implementation of the data-structure-sets in Figure 41.

40 THE ENTITY-RELATIONSHIP APPROACH TO LOGICAL DATABASE DESIGN

types, and finally relationships of the same entity type. The following are the translation rules:

(1) Relationships defined on two different entity types:

(a) The relationship is a one-to-many (or one-to-one) correspondence. For example, the relationship type DEPT-EMP in Figure 43 (a) is a one-to-many correspondence, and can be transformed into the data-structure diagram in Fig-ure 43 (b). Note that the entity types such as DEPT and EMP in the E-R diagram are treated as record types in the data-structure diagram, while the relationship type DEPT-EMP is represented by a data-structure set (an arrow) in the data-structure diagram. Similarly, the relationship type PROJ-MANAGER in Figure 44 (a), which restricts one manager per project but allows multiple projects having the same manager, is represented by an arrow in the data-structure diagram shown in Figure 44 (b).

(b) The relationship is many-to-many correspondence. For instance, the relationship type PROJ-EMP in Figure 45 (a) is a many-to-many correspondence. The corresponding data-structure diagram is shown in Figure 45 (b). Note that the relationship type PROJ-EMP is not translated into an arrow, but rather into a

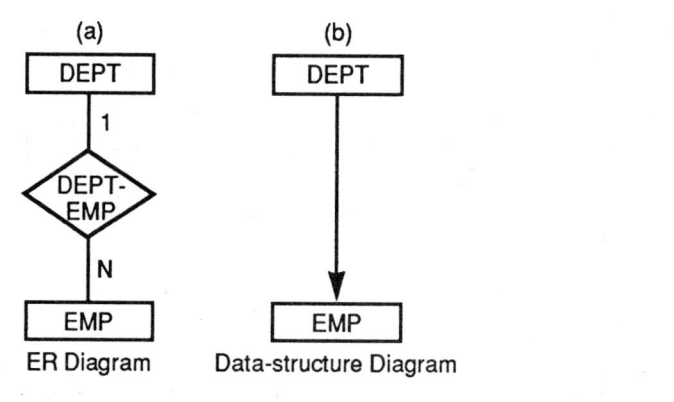

Figure 43.

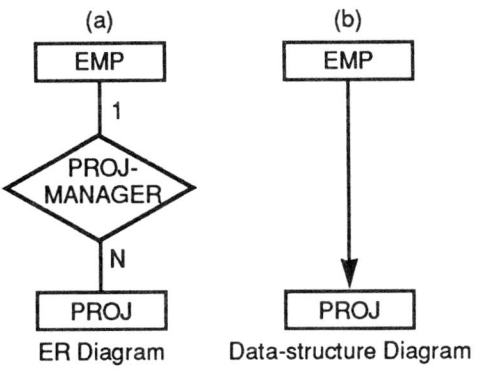

Figure 44.

record type. We may conclude that if a relationship type is a many-to-many correspondence, it will be translated into a record type with two arrows pointing from the related entity record types. The PROJ-EMP record type is usually called a "relationship record type." A similar example is shown in Figure 46. Since the EMP-SKILL relationship type is a many-to-many correspondence, it is translated into a (relationship) record type in the data-structure diagram.

(2) Relationships defined on more than two entity types:

In this case the relationship type in the E-R diagram will be translated into a relationship record type in the data-structure diagram, no matter whether the relationship is a one-to-many or other types of correspondence. For example, the PART-PROJ-SUPP relationship type in Figure 47 (a) is a relationship type defined by three entity types and will be translated into a record type in the data-structure diagram as shown in Figure 47 (b).

(3) Binary relationships defined on the same entity type:

If the binary relationship is a one-to-many correspondence, such as the relationship type MANAGED in Figure 48 (a), it can be transformed into at least two possible data-structure diagrams as shown in Figures 48 (b) and 48 (c). Since

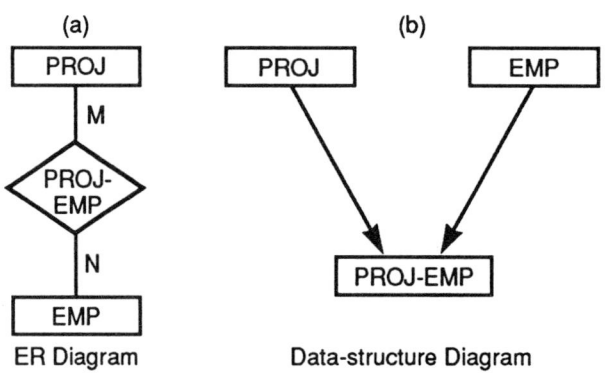

Figure 45.

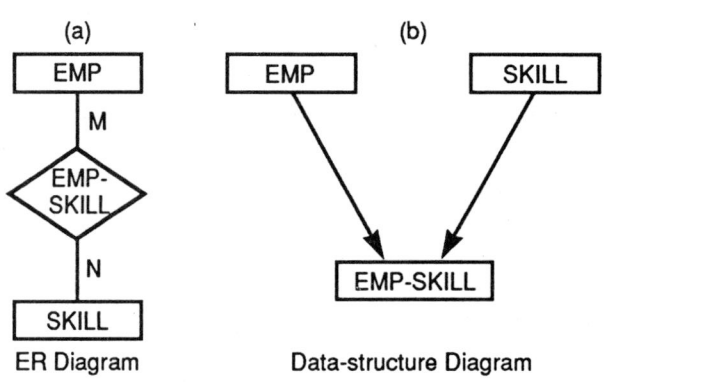

Figure 46.

most Codasyl (network) type database systems do not allow the same record type to be used both as the owner record type and as the member record type of a data-structure set, Figure 48 (b) is illegal. Therefore, we shall use Figure 48 (c) as the data-structure diagram counterpart of the E-R diagram in Figure 48 (a). For binary relationships with other types of correspondence, we shall use the same type of data-structure diagram. For example, MFG-REL is a many-to-many relationship type correspondence, and its equivalent data-structure diagram is shown in Figure 49 (b).

TRANSLATION OF E-R DIAGRAMS INTO DATA-STRUCTURE DIAGRAMS 43

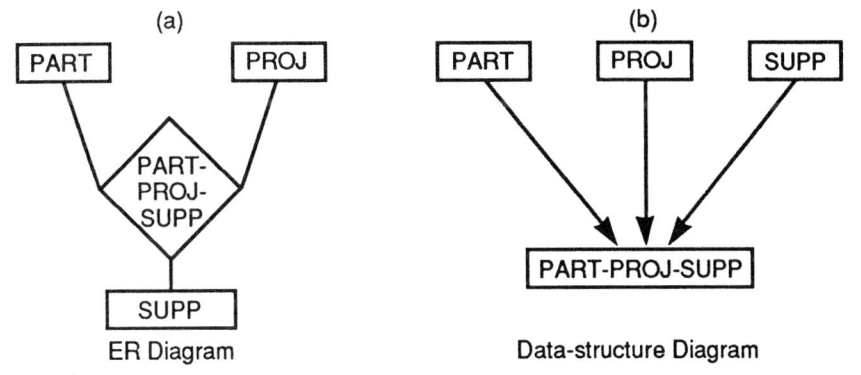

Figure 47.

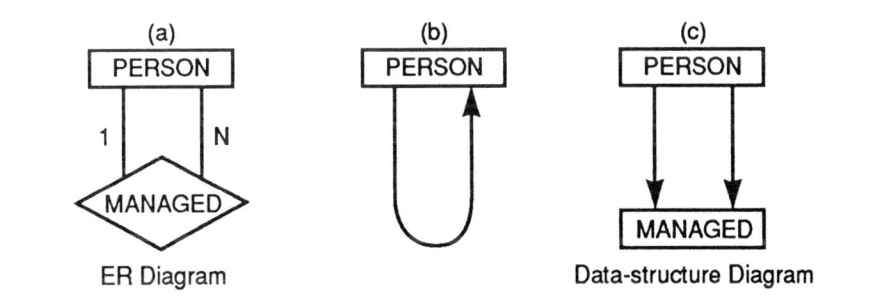

Figure 48.

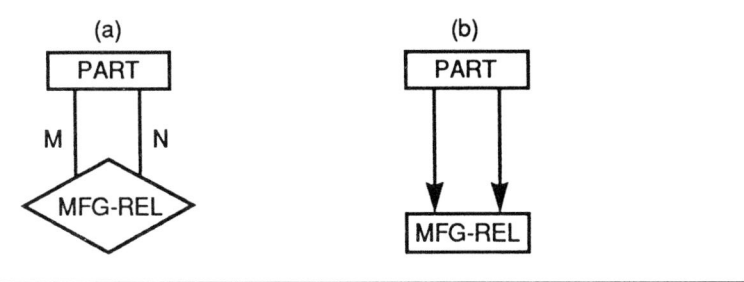

Figure 49.

Steps in Logical Database Design and Examples 5

In this section, we shall first outline the major steps in logical database design and then give three examples of database design using the E-R approach.

5.1 MAJOR STEPS IN LOGICAL DATABASE DESIGN

The entity-relationship approach to database design consists of the following steps:

(1) Identify entity types.

(2) Identify relationship types.

(3) Draw an E-R diagram with entity and relationship types.

(4) Identify value types and attributes.

(5) Translate the E-R diagram into a data-structure diagram.

(6) Design record formats.

5.2 EXAMPLE 1: A MANUFACTURING COMPANY

5.2.1 Identify Entity Types

The first step is to identify entity types of interest to the company. In a manufacturing company, the primary entity types are PART, SUPP (supplier), PROJ, EMP, and DEPT. There are other types of entities which may be of interest to a manufacturing company, but for the sake of simplicity, we shall concentrate on these important entity types.

5.2.2 Identify Relationship Type

We can identify at least the following types of relationships (see Figure 50):

(a) The DEPT-EMP relationship type describes the department affiliation with the employees, and is a one-to-many mapping.

(b) The PROJ-EMP relationship type describes the project's affiliation with the employees and is a many-to-many mapping. That is, each employee can work on more than one project, and each project can involve more than one employee.

(c) The PROJ-MANAGER relationship type identifies the managers of the projects and is a one-to-many mapping. That is, each project has just one manager, but each employee may be associated with more than one project.

(d) The PROJ-SUPP-PART relationship type describes which supplier supplies which part for a particular project and is a many-to-many-to-many three-way mapping. That is, for a particular part, there may be more than one supplier who may supply this part to more than one project. Similarly, each project may use more than one part which may have more than one supplier. Also, each supplier may provide a project with more than one part. One reason that a company might want to seek different suppliers for the same part, used for different projects, is that, in a particular project, the company might need the part immediately and, therefore, may be willing to pay more for it from a local company. In general, this kind of three-way relationship cannot be replaced by three binary relationships, such as PROJ-SUPP, SUPP-PART, and PART-PROJ.

(e) The POTENTIAL-SUPP relationship type keeps a list of potential suppliers of a particular part and is a many-to-many mapping. That is, each part may have more than one potential supplier, and each supplier may be capable of supplying more than one part.

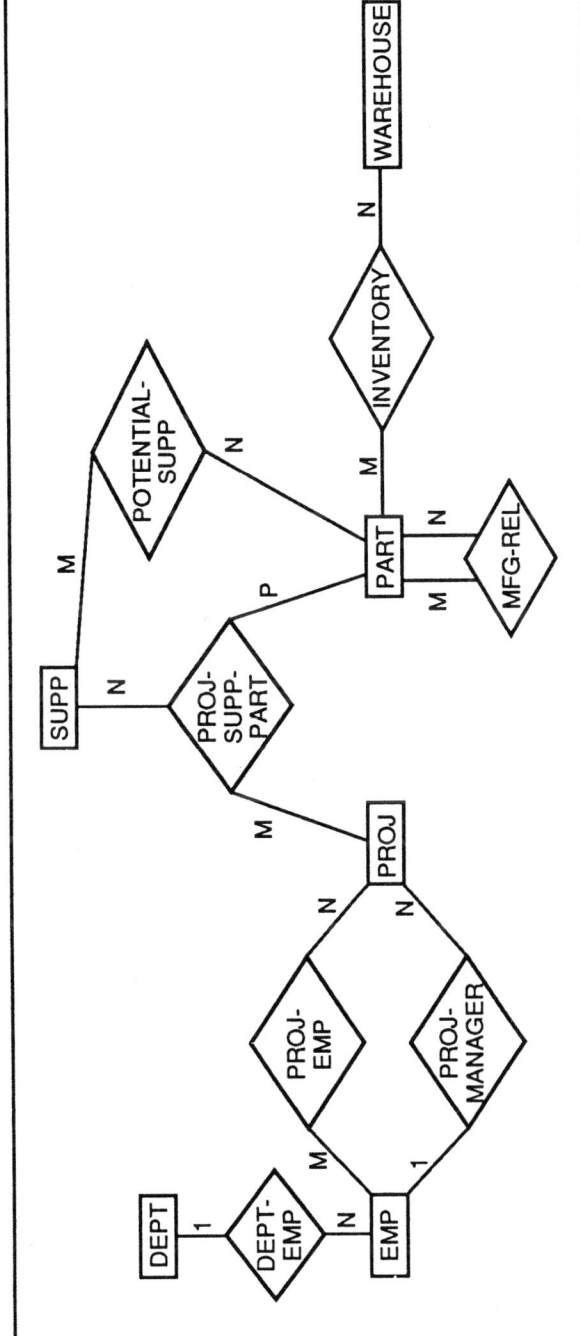

Figure 50. An ER diagram for a manufacturing company.

48 THE ENTITY-RELATIONSHIP APPROACH TO LOGICAL DATABASE DESIGN

(f) The INVENTORY relationship type keeps track of which part is stored in which warehouse and is a many-to-many mapping.

5.2.3 Draw an E-R Diagram with Entity and Relationship Types

The third step is to draw an E-R diagram with the six entity types and seven relationship types mentioned above. Certainly, we may identify entity and relationship types other than those stated above. However, since our purpose is to introduce key concepts of the entity-relationship approach, we shall not go into greater detail than this. The reader of this monograph can add more entity types and relationship types to Figure 50 to meet his own needs.

5.2.4 Identify Value Types and Attributes

The fourth step is to identify the properties of entities and relationships which are of interest to the enterprise. That is, we wish to identify attributes and value types for the entities and relationships in Figure 50.

Let us start with the entity types DEPT and EMP and their relationship DEPT-EMP. Figure 51 illustrates the attributes and value types for DEPT and EMP. The entity types and relationship types are in the upper conceptual domains and the attribute and value types are in the lower conceptual domain. In Figure 51, we have identified the following value types: DEPT-NO, BUDGET, EMP-NO, DATE, SALARY, and PHONE-NO. DEPT has three attributes: DEPT-NO, THIS-YEAR-BUDGET and LAST-YEAR-BUDGET. EMP has five attributes: EMP-NO, BIRTH-DATE, SALARY, HOME-PHONE, and OFFICE-PHONE. Note that attributes may not have the same names as the value types, and that it is possible to have more than one attribute relating to the same value type. For example, THIS-YEAR-BUDGET and LAST-YEAR-BUDGET of DEPT use the same value type BUDGET. Another example is the attributes OFFICE-PHONE and HOME-PHONE of EMP, which use the same value type PHONE-NO. In order to simplify the diagram, we shall omit the attribute names in the diagram if they are the same as the value types. Thus, Figure 52 is a simplified version of Figure 51.

STEPS IN LOGICAL DATABASE DESIGN AND EXAMPLES   49

Next, we shall consider the entity types PROJ and EMP and their relationship types, PROJ-MANAGER and PROJ-EMP. There are five value types: %EFFORT, DATE, PROJ-NO, BUDGET, and PROJ-

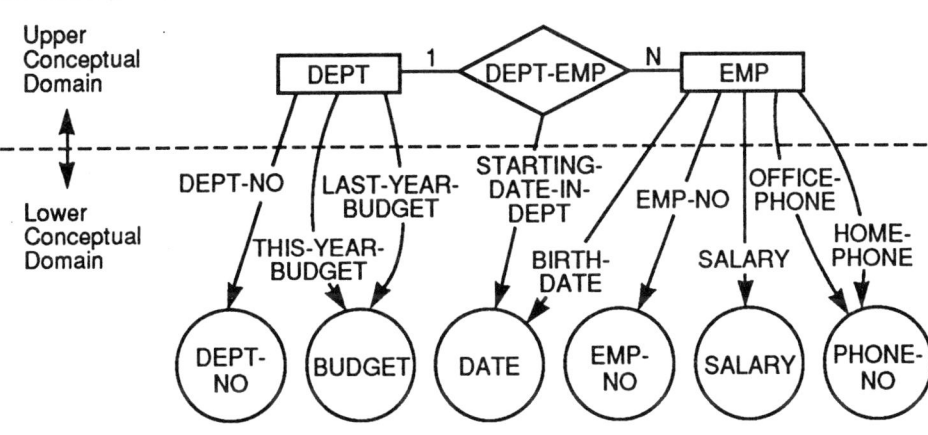

Figure 51. Attributes and value types for DEPT, EMP, and DEPT-EMP.

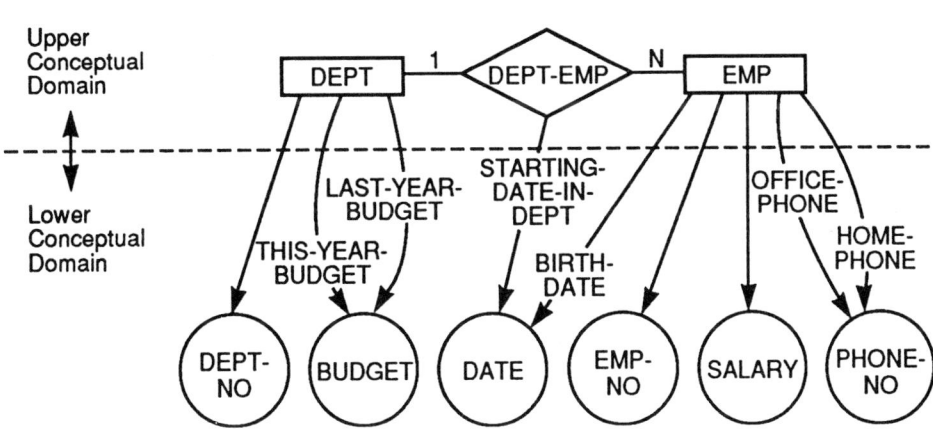

Figure 52. A simplified version of Figure 51.

50 THE ENTITY-RELATIONSHIP APPROACH TO LOGICAL DATABASE DESIGN

NAME. There are also five attributes in Figure 53 (even though some attribute names are omitted in the diagram): %EFFORT, STARTING-DATE-IN-PROJ, PROJ-NO, BUDGET, and PROJ-NAME. Note that the relationship PROJ-EMP has two attributes: STARTING-DATE-IN-PROJ and %EFFORT. The STARTING-DATE-IN-PROJ is the date that the employee started working for a particular project, and the %EFFORT is the percentage of time that an employee is expected to spend on a particular project. Note that the value type BUDGET is the same as the value type BUDGET in Figure 52. Therefore, we may say that attributes can help us to interpret the meaning of values.

Figure 54 illustrates the value types and attributes for entity types SUPP and PART, and relationship types PROJ-SUPP-PART and POTENTIAL-SUPP. The entity SUPP has two attributes: SUPP-NO and ADDRESS. The entity PART has attribute PART NO, WEIGHT, and COLOR. The relationship PROJ-SUPP-PART has attribute QTY,

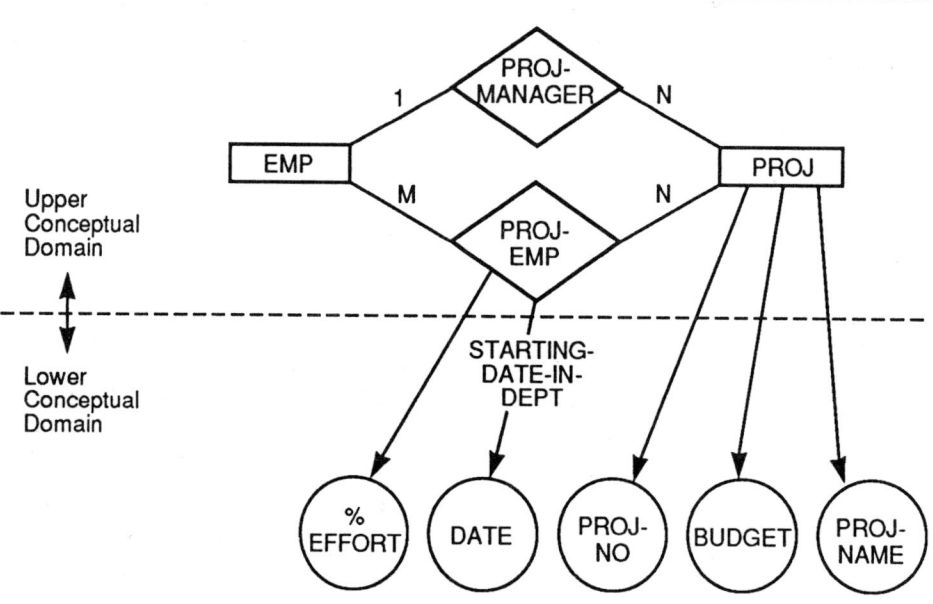

Figure 53. Attributes and value types for PROJ and PROJ-EMP.

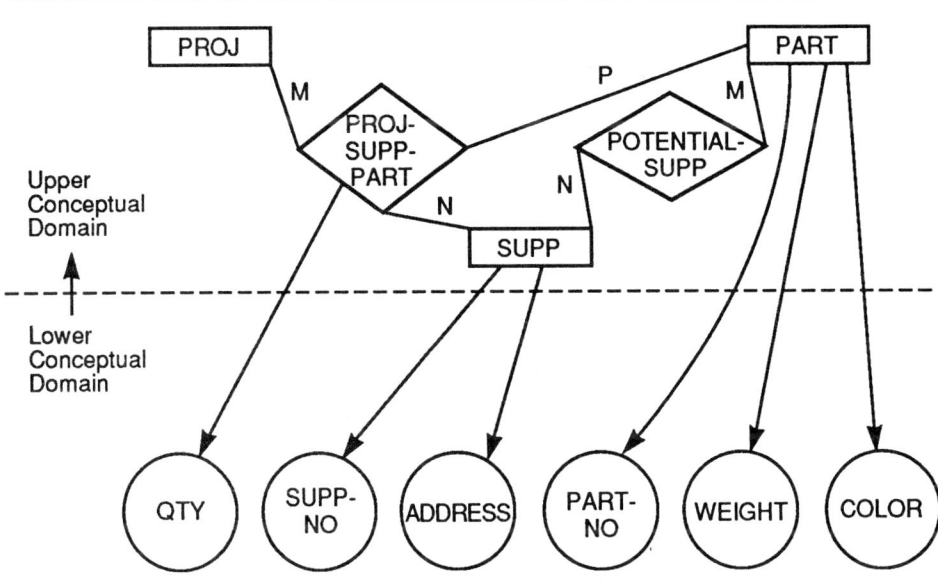

Figure 54. Attributes and value types for SUPP, PART, and PROJ-SUPP-PART.

which is the quantity of a certain part supplied by a certain supplier to a certain project. The relationship POTENTIAL-SUPP does not have an attribute. The attributes of the entity PROJ have already been shown in Figure 53.

Figure 55 shows the attributes and value types of the properties of the WAREHOUSE entity and INVENTORY and MFG-REL relationships. A WAREHOUSE entity has attributes WAREHOUSE-NO and ADDRESS. An INVENTORY relationship has attributes QTY-ON-HAND, which is the quantity of a part stored in a warehouse. A MFG-REL relationship has attribute QTY-FOR-MFG, which is the quantity of a sub-part needed to make a super-part. Note that QTY-ON-HAND and QTY-FOR-MFG share the same value type QTY.

Figures 52-55 illustrate the attributes and value types needed to describe the properties of entities and relationships which may be of interest to a manufacturing company.

52 THE ENTITY-RELATIONSHIP APPROACH TO LOGICAL DATABASE DESIGN

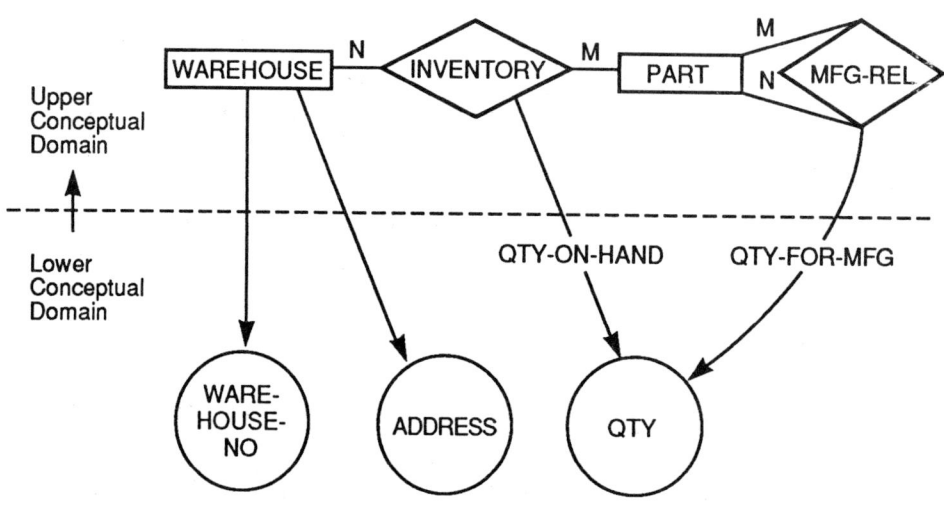

Figure 55. Attributes and value types for WAREHOUSE, INVENTORY, and MFG-REL.

5.2.5 Translate the E-R Diagram into a Data-Structure Diagram

The fifth step is to translate the E-R diagram into a data-structure diagram using the translation rules discussed in Section 4.2.

Consider the E-R diagram in Figure 50. It can be translated into the data-structure diagram shown in Figure 56. All the entity types in the E-R diagram become record types in the data-structure diagram. Since the DEPT-EMP relationship type is a one-to-many mapping, it is translated into a data-structure set (i.e., an arrow) in the data-structure diagram. Similarly, the relationship type PROJ-MANAGER is also a one-to-many mapping and is translated into a data-structure set. Since the relationship type PROJ-EMP is a many-to-many mapping, it is translated into a record type with arrows pointing to it from the related entity record types, EMP and PROJ. Because the relationship type PROJ-SUPP-PART is a many-to-many-to-many three-way mapping, it is translated into a record type. The relationship type MFG-REL is translated into a record type, since it is a relationship type defined on the same entity type. Note that MFG-REL record type in

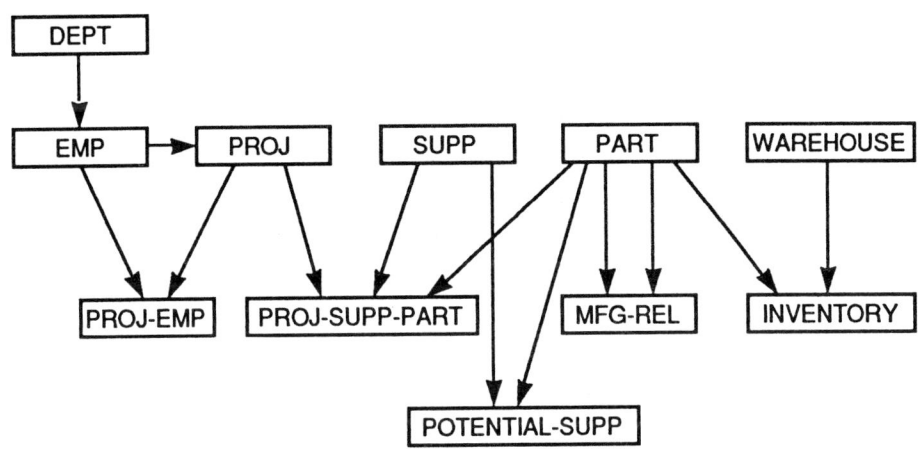

Figure 56. The data-structure diagram derived from the ER diagram in Figure 50.

Figure 42 has two arrows (i.e., data-structure sets) pointing from the same record type PART. Note, also, that the record type PROJ-SUPP-PART is pointed to by three arrows from the related (entity) record types.

5.2.6 Design Record Format

The sixth step is to group attributes of entities and relationships into records and to decide how to implement the data-structure sets (using "chains", "pointer arrays", etc.).

The basic guidelines for grouping attributes into records are:

(1) All the attributes of an entity will be put into the same record type. For example, the attributes of DEPT will be treated as the names of fields in the DEPT record type (see Figures 52 and 57).

(2) If the relationship type is a one-to-many mapping, the attributes of the relationship will be treated as fields in the member record type of the data-structure set. For example, the relationship type DEPT-EMP (Figure 52) is a one-to-many mapping. Its attribute, STARTING-DATE-IN-DEPT,

54 THE ENTITY-RELATIONSHIP APPROACH TO LOGICAL DATABASE DESIGN

will be included as a field in the member record type of the data-structure set (i.e., the EMP record type; see Figures 56 and 58).

(3) If the relationship type is translated into a record type, then the attributes of the relationship will be treated as fields in that record type. For instance, the relationship type PROJ-EMP in Figure 53 is translated into a record type, and the attributes %EFFORT and STARTING-DATE-IN-PROJ become fields in the record type shown in Figure 60.

We can apply these rules to other entity types and relationship types. Since all other entity types and relationship types, except PROJ-MANAGER in Figure 50, are translated directly into record types, the grouping of attributes into record types is straightforward. Figure 53 is translated into Figures 59 and 60. Note that the relationship type PROJ-MANAGER is translated into a data-structure set. Figure 54 is translated into Figures 61-64; Figure 55 is translated into Figures 65 and 66.

After putting all the attributes in the record types, the next question is to decide how to implement the data-structure sets. In this manufacturing company example, we shall use "chains" as the physical implementation of the data-structure sets. That is, we shall use Figures 39 and 42 as the physical implementation of Figures 36 and 40, respectively. From these figures, we may make the following observations on how to implement chain pointers:

(1) If the record is the owner record type of a data-structure set, it should have a pointer to the first member record occurrence.

(2) If the record is a member record type of a data-structure set, it should have a pointer to the next member record occurrence in the chain or to the owner record occurrence, if it is the last record in the chain.

(3) If a record type is involved in multiple data-structure sets, it should contain several pointers, one for each data-structure set.

STEPS IN LOGICAL DATABASE DESIGN AND EXAMPLES   55

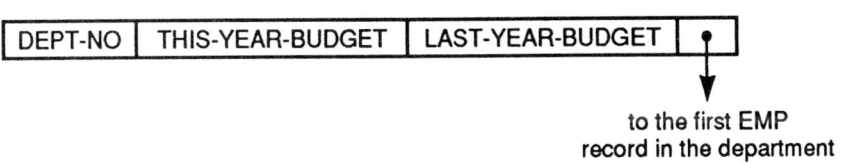

Figure 57. DEPT record.

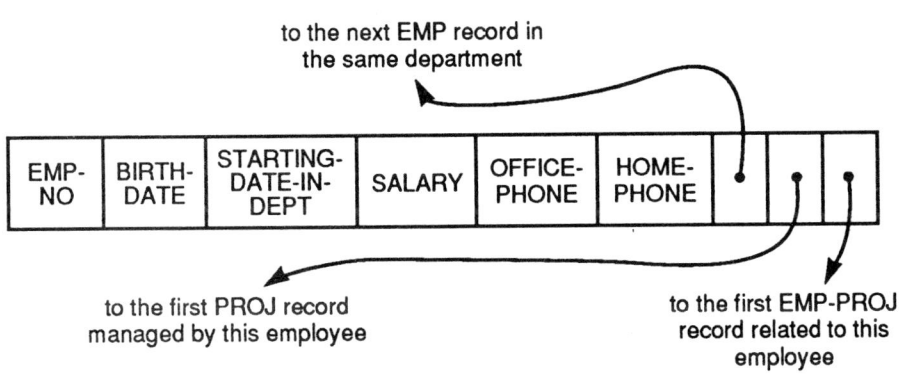

Figure 58. EMP record.

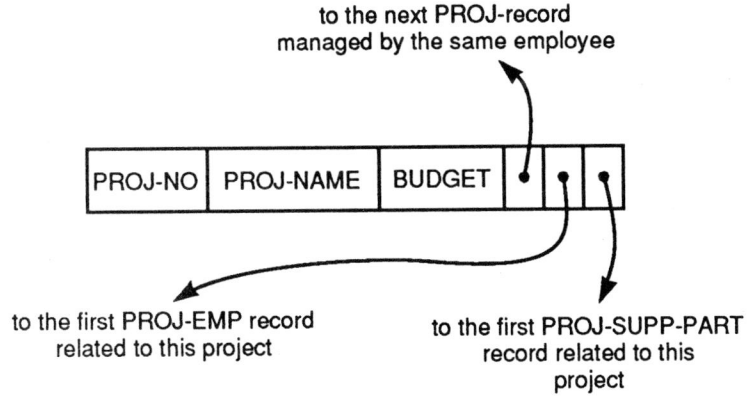

Figure 59. PROJ record.

56 THE ENTITY-RELATIONSHIP APPROACH TO LOGICAL DATABASE DESIGN

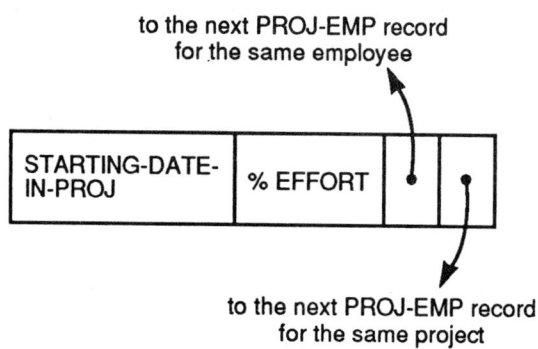

Figure 60. PROJ-EMP record.

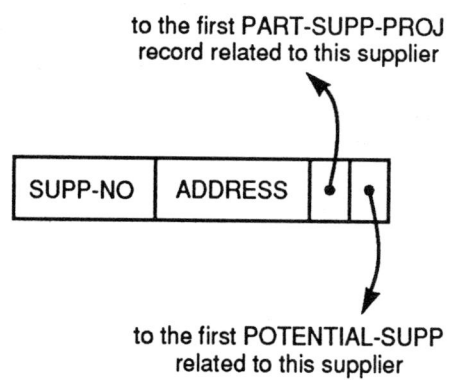

Figure 61. SUPP record.

Using these rules, we can define the pointers in the record types, as shown in Figures 57-66. Let us first consider Figure 57. Since the DEPT record type is the owner record type of a data-structure set, it has a pointer pointing to the first EMP record occurrence in that department. The EMP record type in Figure 58 has three pointers since it is involved in three data-structure sets. Since EMP record type is the member record type of a data-structure set whose owner is the DEPT record type, the EMP record type will keep a pointer to the next EMP record

STEPS IN LOGICAL DATABASE DESIGN AND EXAMPLES   57

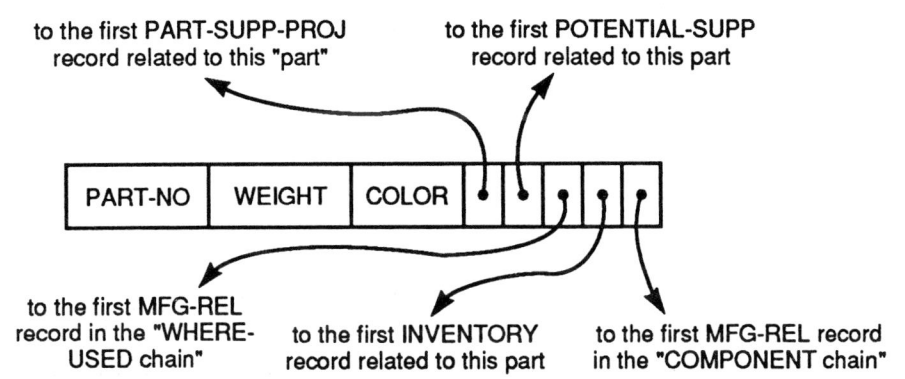

Figure 62. PART record.

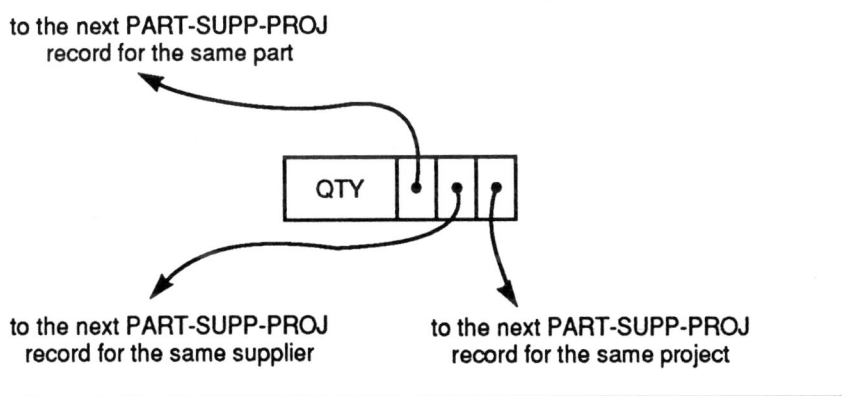

Figure 63. PART-SUPP-PROJ record.

occurrence in the same department. Since EMP record type is the owner record of the data-structure set whose member record type is PROJ, it keeps a pointer to the first PROJ record occurrence managed by this employee. If the employee is not a manager of any project, the value of the pointer is null. Since the EMP record type is also the owner record type of the data-structure set whose member record type is PROJ-EMP, it maintains a pointer to the first PROJ-EMP record occurrence in the chain.

58 THE ENTITY-RELATIONSHIP APPROACH TO LOGICAL DATABASE DESIGN

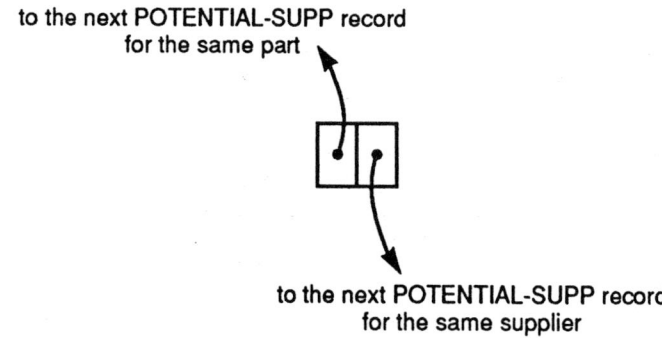

Figure 64. POTENTIAL-SUPP record.

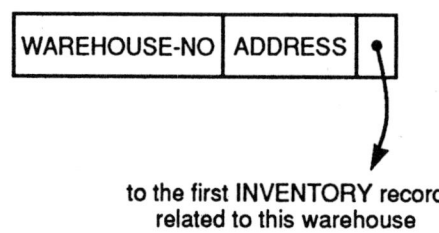

Figure 65. WAREHOUSE record.

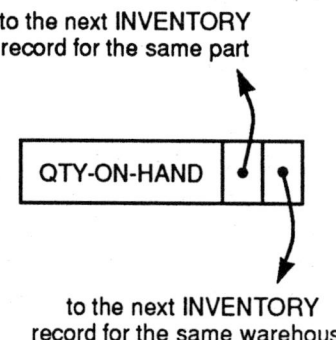

Figure 66. INVENTORY record.

Since PROJ-EMP is the member record type of two data-structure sets, it maintains two pointers; one pointing to the next PROJ-EMP record occurrence for the same employee, and the other pointing to the next PROJ-EMP record occurrence for the same project (see Figures 56 and 60).

Consider a more complicated case: the record type PROJ-SUPP-PART in Figures 56 and 63. Since it is the member record type of three data-structure sets, it has three pointers, one for each chain. Similar explanations can be given for the pointers in other record types.

5.3   EXAMPLE 2: AN ORDER-ENTRY DATABASE

5.3.1   Identity Entity Types

An order-entry handles customers' orders on items which may be stored in certain warehouses. The important entity types are: CUSTOMER, ORDER, LINE, PART, ITEM, and WAREHOUSE (Figure 69). Each "order" has several "lines", each stating the part number and quantity ordered.

5.3.2   Identity Relationship Types

We can identify the following relationship types:

(1) The CUST-ORD relationship type describes which customer places a particular order and is a one-to-many mapping. That is, a customer can place many orders, but each order just has one customer.

(2) The ORD-LINE relationship indicates that LINE entities are existence-dependent and ID-dependent on the corresponding ORDER entities. Each "order" has several "lines", but each "line" belongs to just one "order."

(3) The LINE-PART relationship describes what "part" is put down in this "line" of the "order." It also describes the quantity of the part being ordered. This kind of relationship is a one-to-many mapping. Each "line" contains just one part, but each part can be put in many "lines" (usually in different "orders").

60 THE ENTITY-RELATIONSHIP APPROACH TO LOGICAL DATABASE DESIGN

(4) The INVENTORY relationship keeps track of which part is stored in which warehouse, and is a many-to-many mapping.

5.3.3 Draw an E-R Diagram with Entity and Relationship Types

Figure 67 is an E-R diagram for the given order entry database. Note that two entity types, PART and WAREHOUSE, are already discussed in Example 1. As a matter of fact, it is possible to merge Figures 67 and 50 together to become a large E-R diagram.

5.3.4 Identify Values, Types, and Attributes

Figure 68 shows the attributes and value types for entity types CUSTOMER and ORDER. A CUSTOMER entity has five attributes: CUST-NO, BALANCE, CREDIT-LIMIT, DISCOUNT, and SHIP-TO-ADDRESSES. Each customer may have more than one ship-to-address. An ORDER entity has three attributes: ORDER-NO, SHIP-TO-ADDRESS, and DATE. Each order has just one SHIP-TO-ADDRESS. The relationship CUST-ORD does not have an attribute.

Figure 69 illustrates the attributes and value types of the properties of the LINE entities and the LINE-PART relationships. A LINE entity has one attribute: LINE-NO. A LINE-PART relationship has two attributes: QTY-ORDERED and QTY-OUTSTANDING. The value of the QTY-OUTSTANDING is initially equal to the QTY-ORDERED and gradually reduced to zero when partial shipments are made.

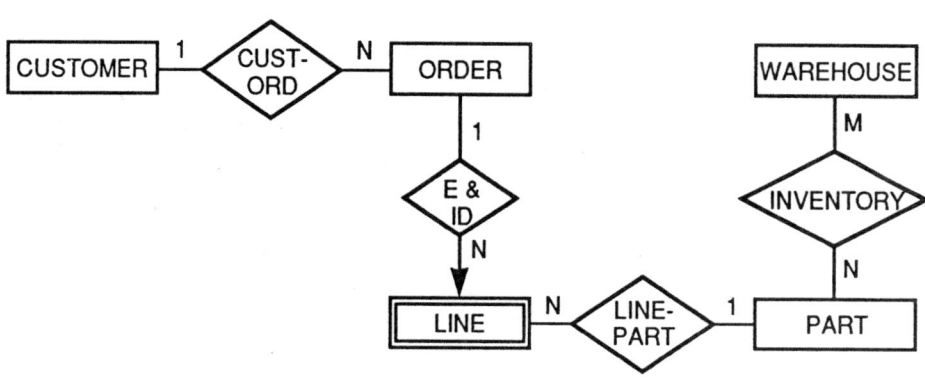

Figure 67. ER diagram for an order-entry database.

The attributes and value types for PART, INVENTORY, and WAREHOUSE can be found in Figures 54 and 55.

5.3.5 Translate the E-R Diagram into a Data-Structure Diagram

Using the translation rules discussed in Section 4.2, the E-R diagram in Figure 67 can be translated into the data-structure diagram shown

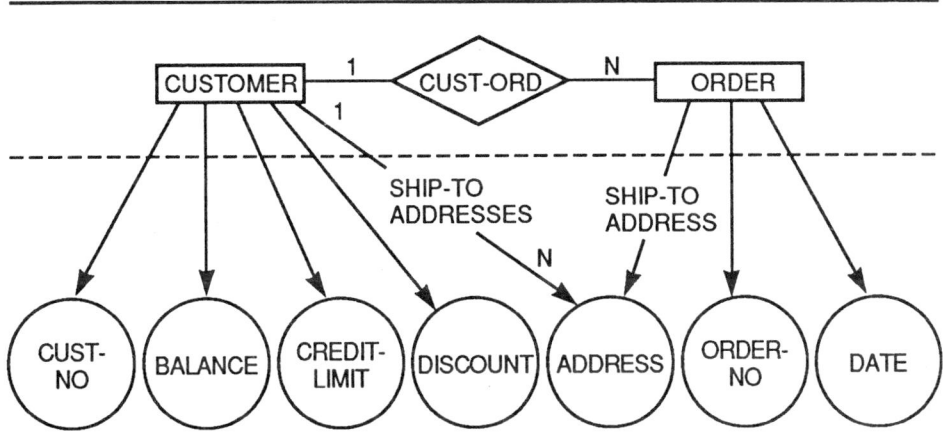

Figure 68. Attributes and value types for CUSTOMER and ORDER.

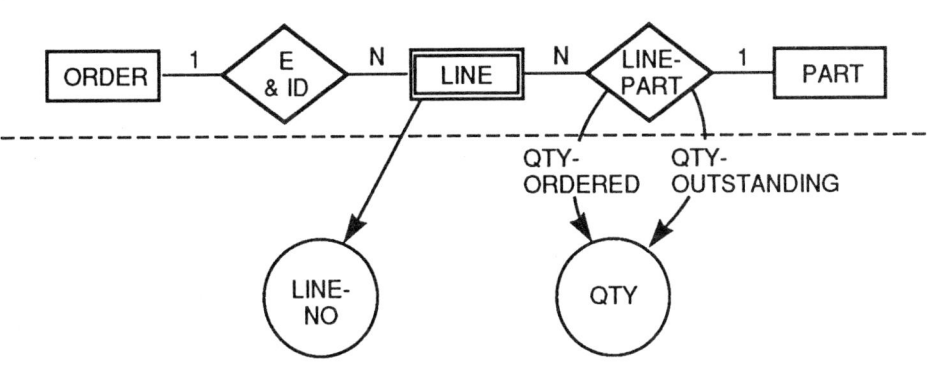

Figure 69. Attributes and value types for LINE and LINE-PART.

62 THE ENTITY-RELATIONSHIP APPROACH TO LOGICAL DATABASE DESIGN

in Figure 70. All the entity types become record types in the data-structure diagram. Since the CUST-ORD, ORD-LINE, and LINE-PART relationship types are one-to-many mapping, they are translated into data-structure sets in the data-structure diagram. Since the relationship type INVENTORY is a many-to-many mappings, it is translated into a record type.

5.3.6 Design Record Format

Figures 71 to 74 illustrate the record formats for the four record types CUSTOMER, ORDER, LINE, and PART in Figure 70. The LINE record contains not only the attributes of LINE entity, but also the attributes of LINE-PART relationships (see Figures 69 and 73). In this order-entry database example, we also choose "chains" as the physical implementation of the data-structure sets. The record formats for record types WAREHOUSE and INVENTORY are shown in Figures 65 and 66. Note that if we merge Figures 56 and 70 together, we have to redesign the record format for PART record; that is, to merge Figure 62 with Figure 74.

5.4 EXAMPLE 3: A LIBRARY DATABASE

5.4.1 Identify Entity Types

A library wants to keep track of its books and also provide a computerized system for searching for the books by categories, keywords

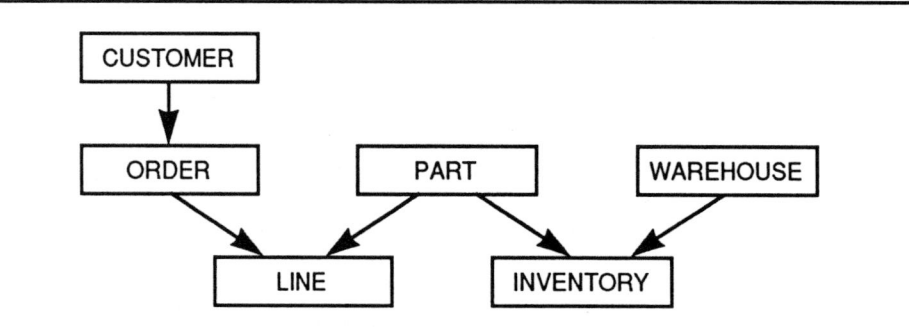

Figure 70. The data-structure diagram derived from the ER diagram in Figure 67.

STEPS IN LOGICAL DATABASE DESIGN AND EXAMPLES   63

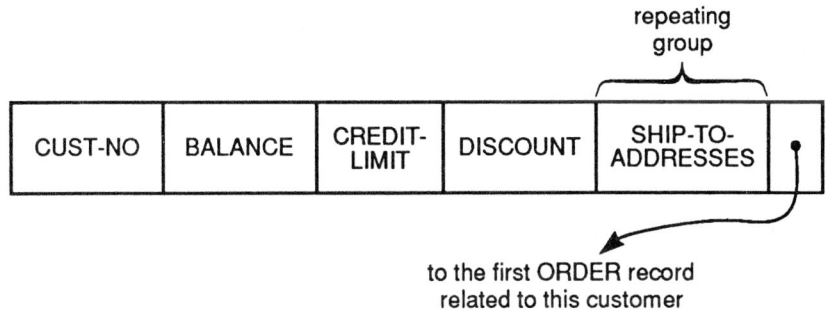

Figure 71. CUSTOMER record.

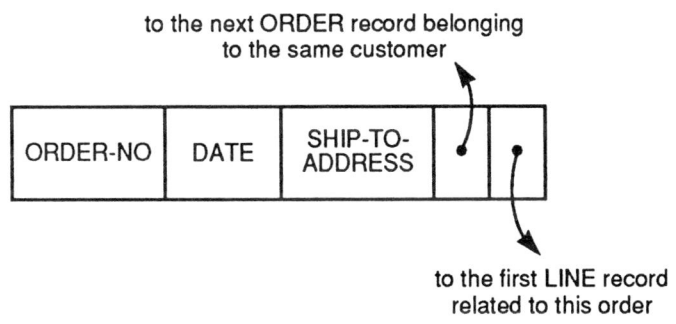

Figure 72. ORDER record.

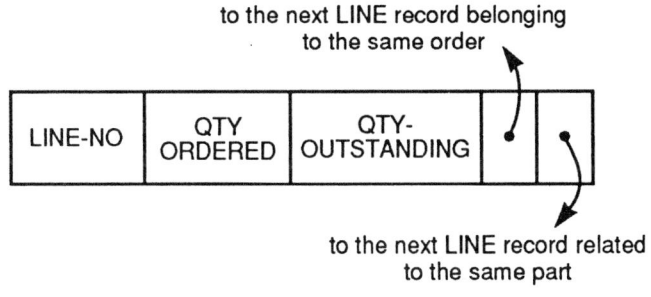

Figure 73. LINE record.

64 THE ENTITY-RELATIONSHIP APPROACH TO LOGICAL DATABASE DESIGN

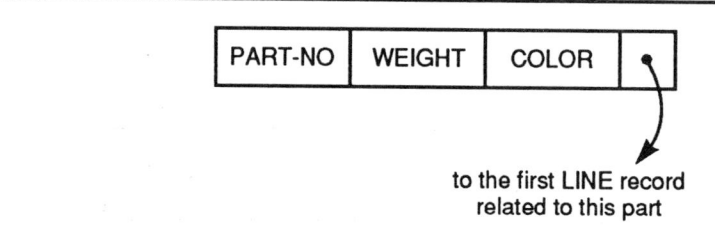

Figure 74. PART record.

or authors. Important entity types are: BOOK, AUTHOR, KEYWORD, CATEGORY, and EMPLOYEE (see Figure 75).

5.4.2 Identify Relationship Types

There are two kinds of relationships between AUTHOR entities and BOOK entities. One is the PRINCIPAL-AUTHORSHIP, and the other is the CO-AUTHORSHIP (see Figure 75). Each book has only one principal author, but an author may be the principal author of many books. On the other hand, each book may have several co-authors (in addition to the principal author), and each author can be the co-author of many books. There are two kinds of relationships between CATEGORY entities and BOOK entities: one is PRIMARY-DIRECTORY, and the other is SECONDARY-DIRECTORY. Each book belongs to only one primary category but may belong to several secondary categories. For example, a book related to "physical chemistry" may have "chemistry" as its primary category and "physics" as its secondary category. There is also a relationship type called SUBCATEGORY which is defined between CATEGORY entities; that is, each category can be divided into subcategories. For example, "science" can be divided into "physics," "chemistry," mathematics," etc. Similarly, there exist two kinds of relationships between KEYWORD entities and BOOK entities: one is the PRIMARY-CLASSIFICATION, and the other is the SECONDARY-CLASSIFICATION. Each keyword can be divided into several subkeys. In addition, each keyword can have several synonyms. For example, "computer memory," "main memory," and "core memory" are synonyms. There exist two kinds of relationships between EMPLOYEE entities and BOOK entities: one is BORROWING, and the other is REQUESTING. Each employee may borrow several books, but

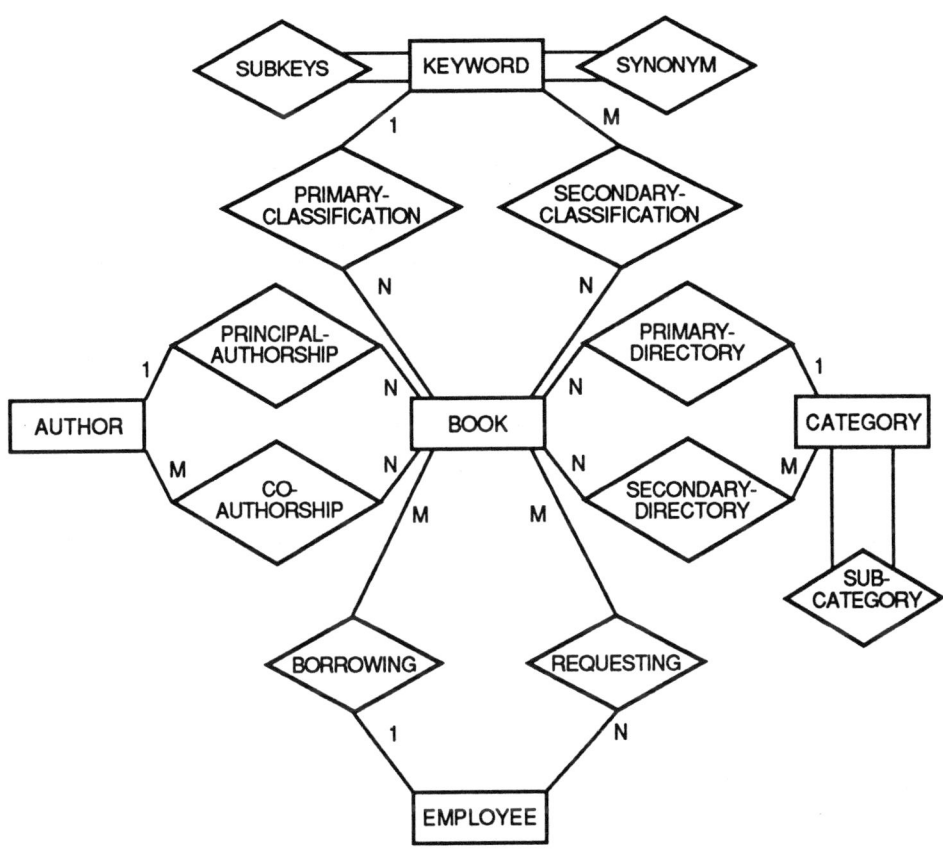

Figure 75. An ER diagram for a library database.

a book usually is signed out by only one employee. If an employee cannot find a book in the library, he can request the library to hold it for him when it is returned. The REQUESTING relationship is a many-to-many mapping.

5.4.3 Draw an E-R Diagram

The E-R Diagram for the library database is shown in Figure 75. Note that we can combine Figure 75 with Figure 50 and Figure 67 to obtain a large E-R diagram.

5.4.4 Identify Attributes and Value Types

Figure 76 shows the attributes and value types for AUTHOR and BOOK. An AUTHOR entity has two attributes: NAME and BIRTH-DATE. A BOOK entity has four attributes: PUBLICATION-DATE, TITLE, EDITION, and LIBRARY-OF-CONGRESS-NO.

Figure 77 illustrates the attributes and value types for CATEGORY and SECONDARY-DIRECTORY. Each CATEGORY entity has a name such as "physics" or "chemistry." A SECONDARY-DIRECTORY relationship has an attribute called RELEVANCE, which is a numerical value (such as 0.1, 0.55, 0.9) assigned by a librarian to indicate the degree of relevance between a book and a secondary category. The primary category is assumed to have 1.0 as the degree of relevance. The concept of "RELEVANCE" can narrow the scope of searches in the database. Similarly, a SECONDARY-CLASSIFICATION relationship in Figure 78 also has an attribute called RELEVANCE.

The attributes and value types for EMPLOYEE, BORROWING, and REQUESTING are shown in Figure 79. An EMPLOYEE has two attributes: EMP-NO and NAME. A BORROWING relationship has two attributes: CHECK-OUT-DATE and DUE-DATE. This information can help the librarian figure out which book is overdue. A REQUESTING relationship has an attribute called REQUESTED-DATE, which provides the necessary information for the librarian to assign the book to the appropriate employee when the book becomes available.

5.4.5 Translate the E-R Diagram into a Data-Structure Diagram

Using the translation rules discussed in Section 4.2, the E-R diagram in Figure 75 can be translated into the data-structure diagram shown in Figure 80. All relationship types which are one-to-many mappings are translated into data-structure sets (arrows). For example, the PRINCIPAL-AUTHORSHIP relationship type is translated into an arrow. All relationship types which are many-to-many mappings are translated into record types. For instance, the CO-AUTHORSHIP relationship type is translated into a record type pointed at by two arrows (one from the AUTHOR record type and the other from the BOOK record type).

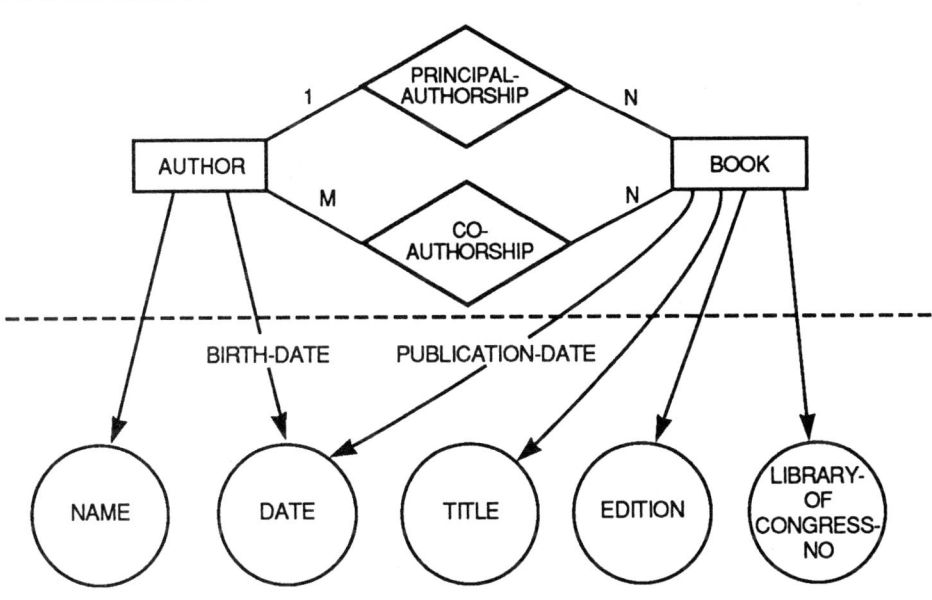

Figure 76. Attributes and value types for AUTHOR and BOOK.

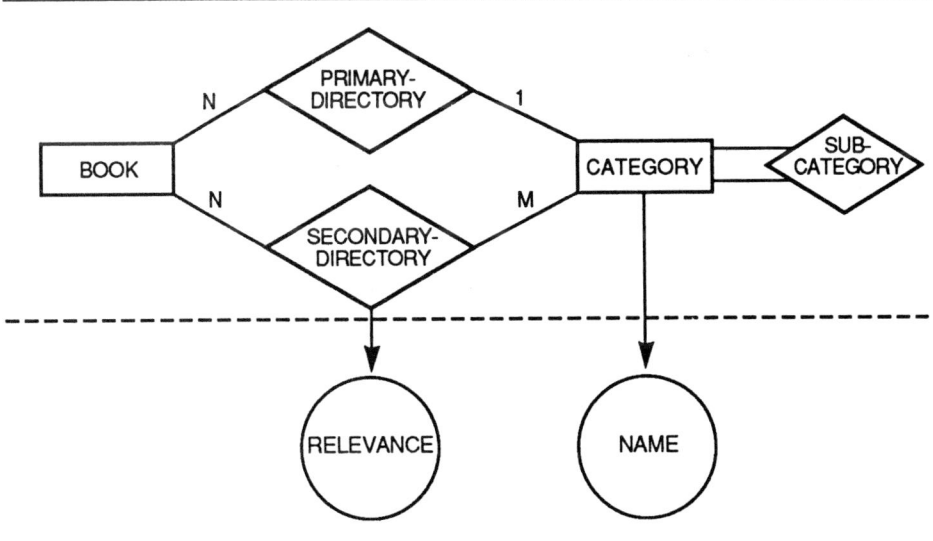

Figure 77. Attributes and value types for CATEGORY and SECONDARY-DIRECTORY.

68 THE ENTITY-RELATIONSHIP APPROACH TO LOGICAL DATABASE DESIGN

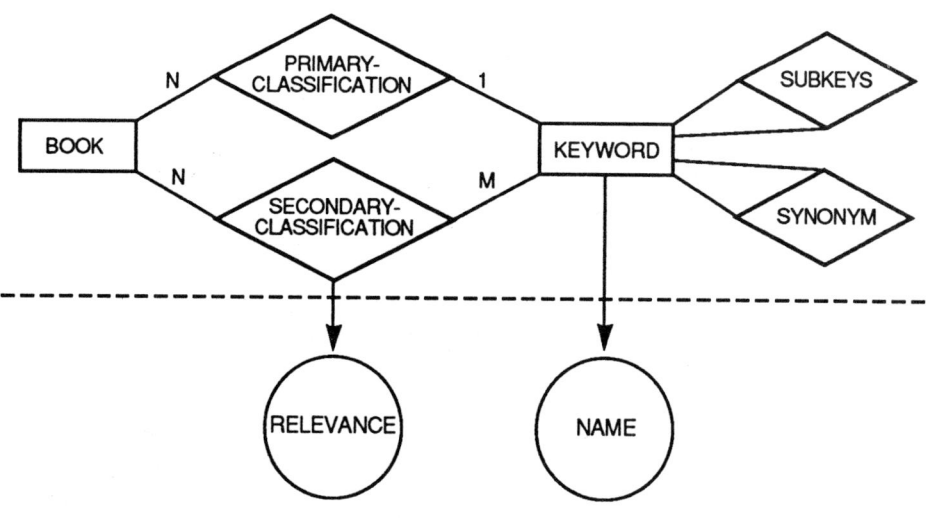

Figure 78. Attributes and value types for KEYWORD and SECONDARY-CLASSIFICATION.

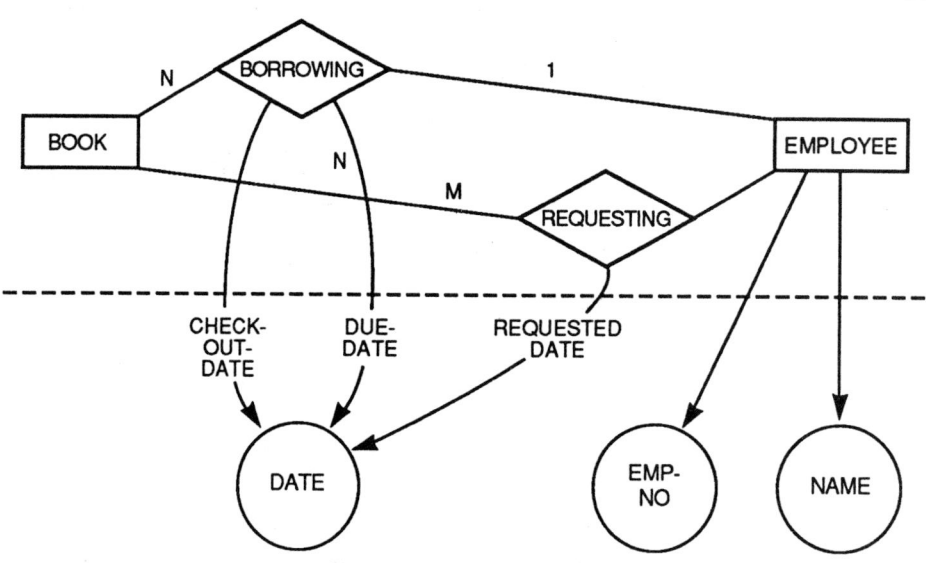

Figure 79. Attributes and value types for EMPLOYEE, BORROWING, and REQUESTING.

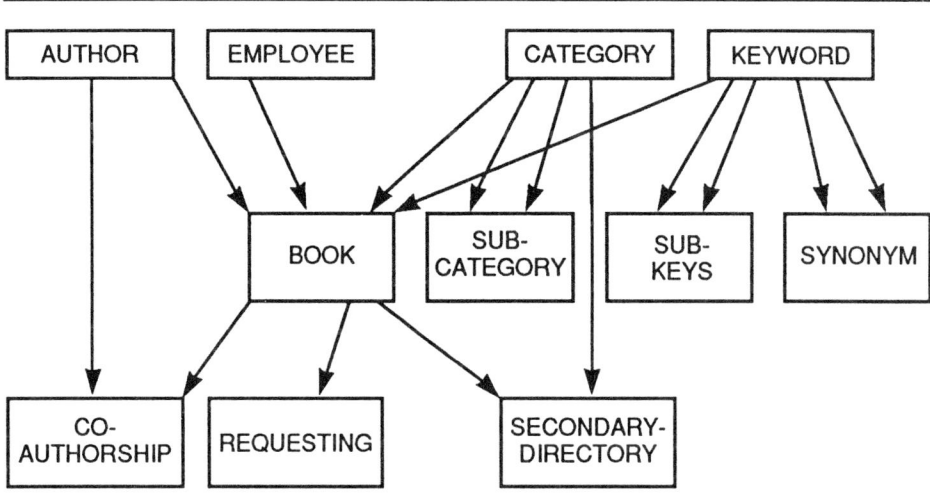

Figure 80. A data-structure diagram derived from the ER diagram in Figure 75.

The relationship types defined between entities of the same type are also translated into record types. For example, the relationship type SUBKEYS is translated into a record type.

5.4.6 Design Record Format

The formats of the records are similar to those discussed in the previous two database examples. Therefore, we omit the discussion here.

Other Considerations In Logical Database Design 6

6.1 OTHER TRANSLATION RULES FROM E-R DIAGRAMS TO DATA-STRUCTURE DIAGRAMS

The translation rules from E-R Diagrams to Data-Structure Diagrams discussed in Section 4.2 are commonly used, but are not the only rules. We may use a simple rule which translates all relationship types into record types, no matter what types of mapping they are (many-to-many, one-to-many, etc.). Using this rule, the E-R diagram in Figure 50 would be translated into Figure 81 instead of Figure 56. The E-R diagram in Figure 67 would be translated into Figure 82 instead of Figure 70. Note that all relationship types are translated into record types except the "existent or ID dependent" relationship types. For example, the relationship type between ORDER and LINE in Figure 67 is translated into a data-structure set (an arrow) in Figure 67.

Using this simplified rule, the resultant data-structure diagram will be more complicated and may be less efficient in retrieval and updating. However, it may provide a higher level of data independence. That is, programs and database structures need not be changed when a particular relationship type changes from a one-to-many mapping to a many-to-many mapping. This change in types of mappings will convert a data-structure set into a record type, or vice versa, if the translation rules discussed in Section 4.2 are used, but no change is needed if the simplified rule discussed in this section is used.

72 THE ENTITY-RELATIONSHIP APPROACH TO LOGICAL DATABASE DESIGN

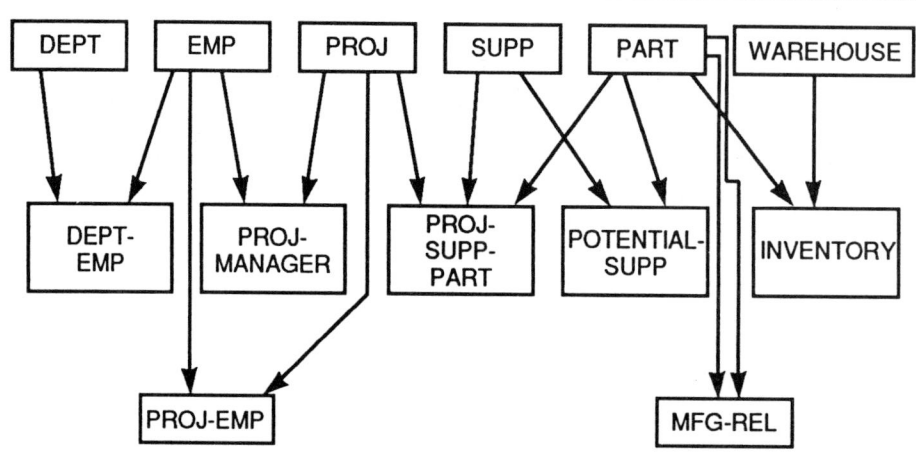

Figure 81. Another data-structure diagram derived from the ER diagram in Figure 50.

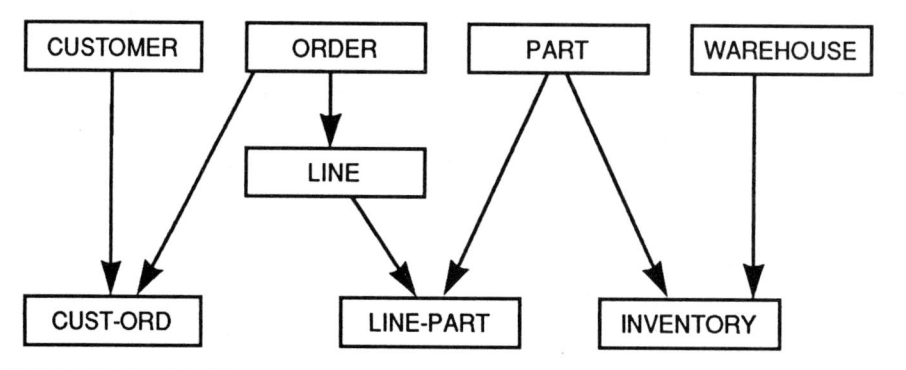

Figure 82. Another data-structure diagram derived from the ER diagram in Figure 67.

6.2 MODIFY THE DATA-STRUCTURE DIAGRAM FOR PERFORMANCE AND STORAGE REASONS

After we obtain data-structure diagrams from E-R diagrams using the translation rules, we may want to modify them to get better system performance or better utilization of storage space. For example, we may split the EMP record in Figures 56, 58 and 81 into two records. One is the EMP-MASTER record which contains fields EMP-NO, BIRTH-DATE, and SALARY (see Figure 83). The other is the EMP-DETAIL record which contains the fields STARTING-DATE-IN-DEPT, OFFICE-PHONE, and HOME-PHONE (see Figure 84). Note that a pointer is needed to connect the occurrence of these two record types. The data-structure diagrams in Figures 56 and 81 will be modified by incorporating Figure 85. One of the reasons for splitting a record into two or three records is to improve the retrieval performance. For example, we would expect that the fields in the EMP-MASTER record will be used more often than the fields in the EMP-DETAIL record. Since we do not want to retrieve the data which is not needed, it would be a good idea to split the record into two records. Another reason to split a record into two records is due to the limitation of the record size. In some cases due to hardware/software limitations, it may be preferable to limit the record size to a fixed length (say 256 bytes). If a "conceptual" record is larger than the maximum length of a record, the "conceptual" record may have to be split into two or more records.

Another common practice is to factor out the repeating groups. For example, the SHIP-TO-ADDRESSES in Figures 68 and 71 is a repeating group (i.e., there are may data values for this attribute). We

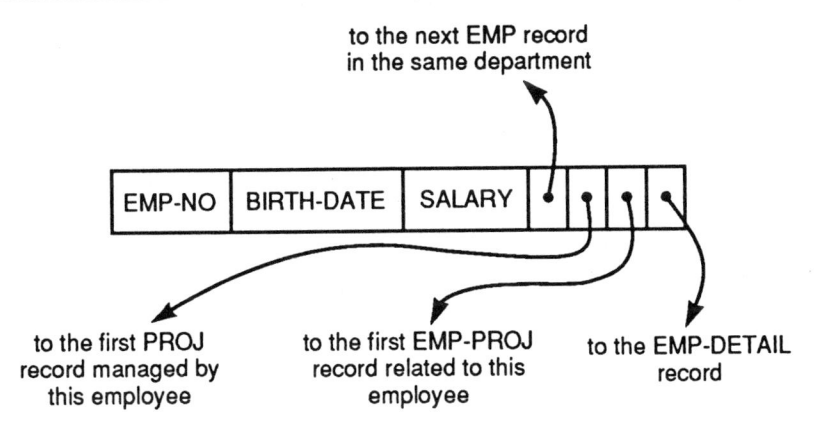

Figure 83. EMP-MASTER record.

74 THE ENTITY-RELATIONSHIP APPROACH TO LOGICAL DATABASE DESIGN

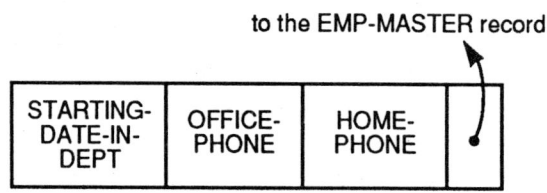

Figure 84. EMP-DETAIL record.

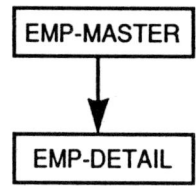

Figure 85. Data-structure diagram for EMP-MASTER and EMP-DETAIL.

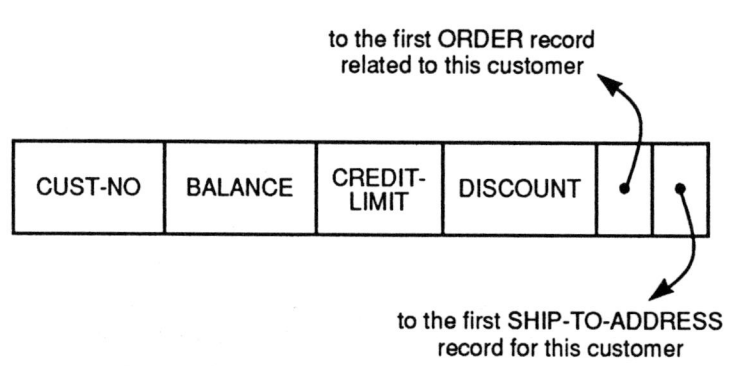

Figure 86. A "new" CUSTOMER record.

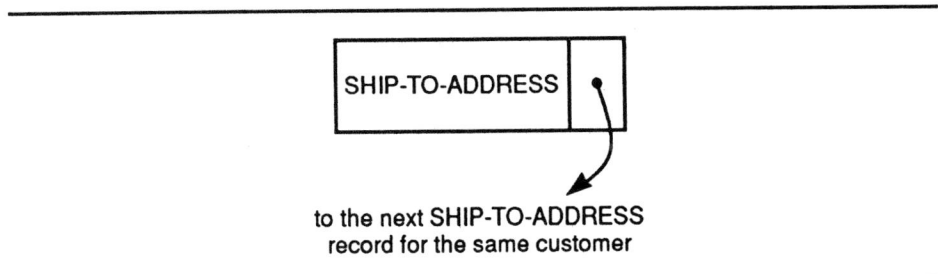

Figure 87. SHIP-TO-ADDRESS record.

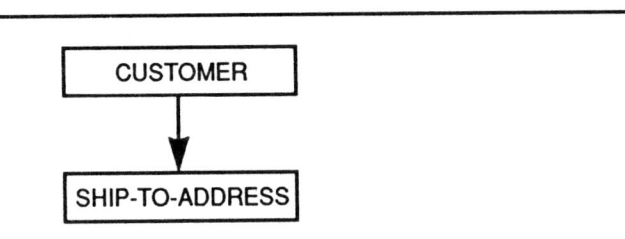

Figure 88. A data-structure diagram for CUSTOMER and SHIP-TO-ADDRESS.

can move this field out and put it into a new record called SHIP-TO-ADDRESS (see Figures 86 and 87). The data-structure diagrams in Figures 70 and 82 will be modified by incorporating Figure 88 into the diagrams.

Note that an E-R diagram may be translated into many different data-structure diagrams to meet different data processing needs. Therefore, we recommend that the database designer start with an E-R diagram and then translate it into a data-structure diagram suitable for his environment.

Design of Hierarchical Databases   7

In hierarchical database systems such as IBM's IMS, data will be organized into hierarchies of records (see Figure 7). In this section, we shall give a brief discussion on how to use the E-R approach for the design of hierarchical databases.

7.1 TRANSLATION RULES

Since the hierarchical relationship types allow only one-to-many mappings, we have to translate relationship types with many-to-many mappings into hierarchical structures. There are at least five possible logical data structures for the E-R diagram about PROJ-EMP in Figure 89. These five logical data structures are listed as follows:

(1) The PROJ record type is treated as a "child-record" (or "subordinate-record") for EMP record type (see Figure 90). This logical data structure will be efficient for certain types of queries but not efficient for other types of queries. For example, if we want to find all the employees associated with a particular project, we may have to do an exhaustive search of the whole database.

(2) The EMP record type is treated as a "child-record" for PROJ record type (see Figure 91). An exhaustive search of the whole database would be needed if we want to find all the projects associated with a particular employee.

78 THE ENTITY-RELATIONSHIP APPROACH TO LOGICAL DATABASE DESIGN

(3) Since neither the logical data structure in Figure 90 nor the one in Figure 91 can be efficient for all types of queries, we may want to maintain two databases as shown in Figure 92. But this requires the maintenance of redundant data.

(4) In IMS, we may choose the logical data structure in Figure 93 so that EMP record type will be the "physical parent" of PROJ-EMP, and PROJ record type will be the "logical parent."

(5) An alternative in IMS is to make the EMP record type the "logical parent" instead of the "physical parent" of PROJ-EMP record type (see Figure 94).

7.2 EXAMPLE

For the E-R diagram of the order-entry database (Figure 67), we may derive many possible hierarchical logical structures. One possible structure is shown in Figure 95 in which the LINE record type is the "physical child" of the ORDER record type and the "logical child" of the PART record type.

Note that Figure 95 may be modified (i.e., by splitting or merging record types) to meet performance or storage requirements.

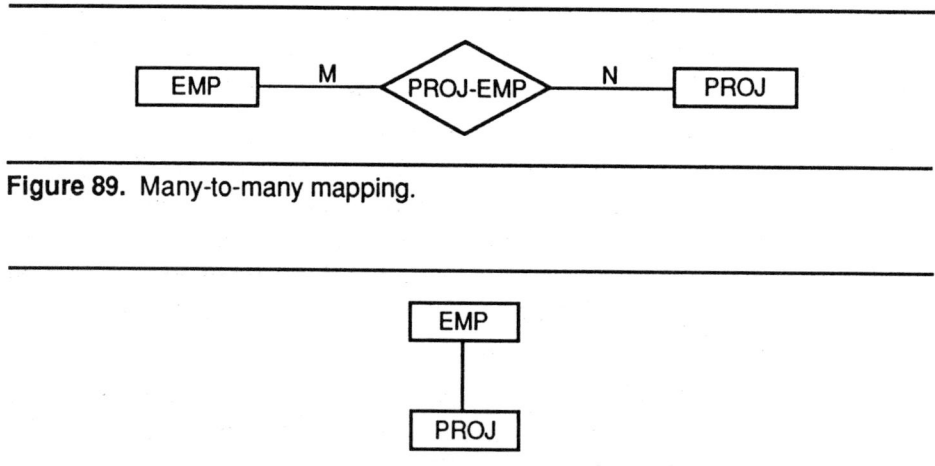

Figure 89. Many-to-many mapping.

Figure 90. PROJ as a child-record for EMP.

DESIGN OF HIERARCHICAL DATABASES 79

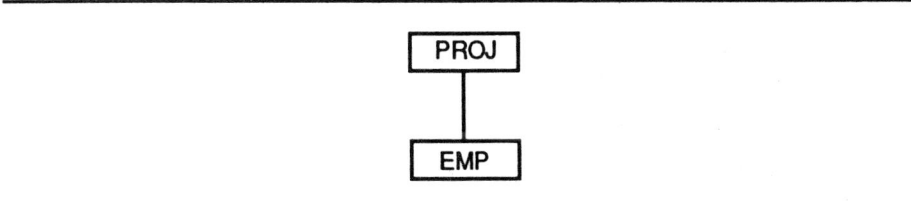

Figure 91. EMP as a child-record for PROJ.

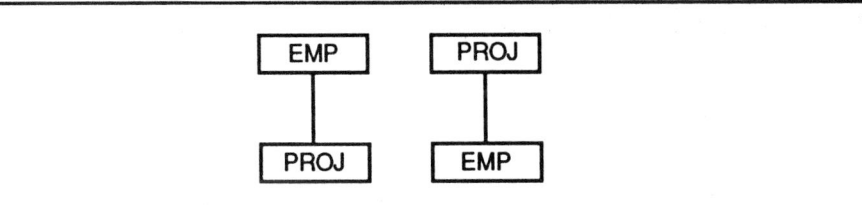

Figure 92. Maintaining two databases.

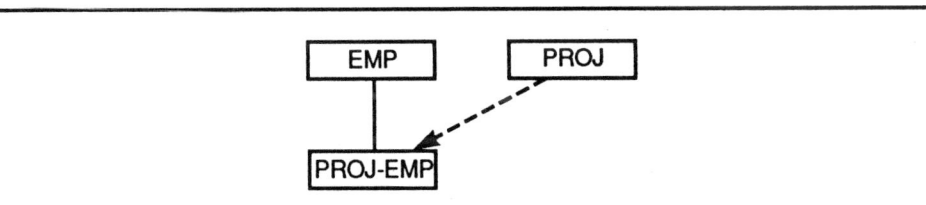

Figure 93. PROJ as the "logical parent" of PROJ-EMP.

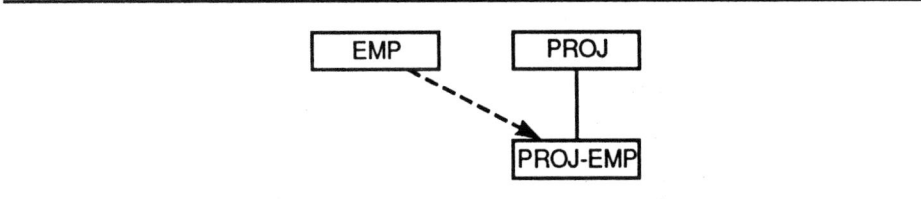

Figure 94. EMP as the "logical parent" of PROJ-EMP.

80 THE ENTITY-RELATIONSHIP APPROACH TO LOGICAL DATABASE DESIGN

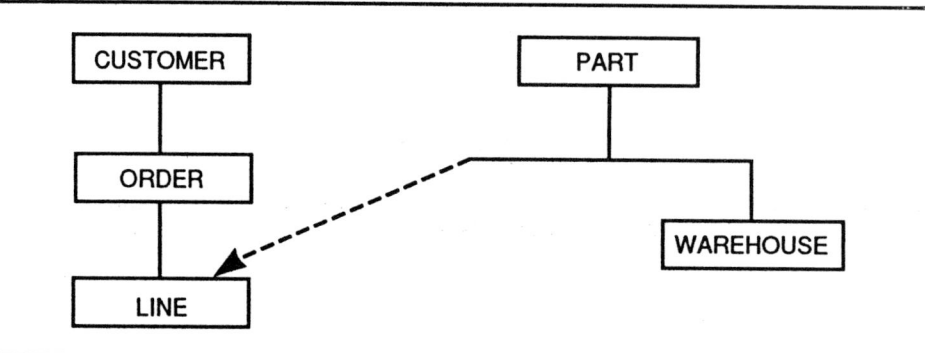

Figure 95. A hierarchical database for the ER diagram in Figure 67.

Final Remarks   8

In this monograph, we have outlined a new approach in logical database design: the Entity-Relationship Approach. The approach base has been tested in real-world environments and has been found both easy-to-understand and easy-to-use. In particular, the E-R diagram has been found to be a valuable and effective communication tool between EPD people and non-EDP people.

One of our current projects at M.I.T. is to develop detailed standardized E-R diagrams for various types of industries such as manufacturing, banking, retailing, etc., which can be used in assisting either database design or information system planning. Several papers relevant to the E-R approach are listed in the references. Any suggestions to improve the E-R approach will be appreciated.

References

(1) CHEN, Peter, P.S., "The Entity Relationship Model: Towards a Unified View of Data," *ACM Transaction on Database Systems*, Vol. 1, No. 1, (March 1976), pages 9-36.

(2) CHEN, Peter, P.S., "The Entity-Relationship Model: A Basis for the Enterprise View of Data," *AFIPS Conference Proceedings*, Vol. 46, AFIPS Press, N.J., (1977 National Computer Conference), pages 77-84.

(3) HO, Thomas I.M., "New Perspectives for Information Systems Education," *AFIPS Conference Proceedings*, Vol. 46, AFIPS Press, N.H., (1977 National Computer Conference), pages 569-574.

(4) HO, Thomas, I.M., "Data Base Concepts for Systems Analysis," *Purdue University, Computer Sciences Department Technical Report*, November 1976.

(5) Moulin, P.J., Randon, M. Teboul, et al., "Conceptual Model as a Database Design Tool," *Proc. IFIP TC-2 Working Conference.*, January 1976, Black Forest, Germany, pages 459-479.

(6) TOZER, E.E., "Database Systems Analysis and Design," *Technical Report, Software Sciences Limited*, England, April 1976.